Table of Contents

INTRODUCTION	4
SIR LANCELOT TAKES A NAP	7
A KNIGHT'S FUNERAL	11
LOST	16
FROZEN KNIGHT	26
RIDING LESSONS	34
??!!WHAT'S THAT SMELL!!??	43
CRAZY KID	49
FRIER TUCK	59
FIRST LOVE	63
PARATROOOPER SCHOOL	74
BIOLOGY 101	79
LOST AGAIN	86
SKUNKED	99
EENY INY OVER	108
HIDE AND SEEK	117
I WAS WRONG ABOUT GIRLS	126
SIR LANCELOT GOES TO SCHOOL	136
YOU'RE NOT DEAD UNTIL YOU'RE DEAD	142
SUNDAY SCHOOL	149
BLACKIE	155
BOUNTY HUNTER	162
THE RAT KILLING	168
WALTER	180
PETUNIA	188
DRIVING WITH NO LICENSE	196
TO THE DUMP	206
WALTER TAKES A BATH	215
GROOM	225
KIDS LIKE BALD	233
A HERO DIES	238
LEGACY	246
INTERIOR DECORATOR	251
WHAT'S WRONG WITH MERLIN?	257
THE KINGDOM CRUMBLES	268
ABOUT THE AUTHOR	274

AUTHOR'S NOTES

I intended to write a whimsical tale reflecting the childhood of a bright kid growing up in hard times. I read my little tale and discovered that I accidentally wrote a philosophy book with lessons for everyone except teenagers. It is useless to tell teenagers anything as they are busy trying out the things they learned earlier in life as well as breaking free of parental control. It is interesting to watch them copy their parent's values even as they express disdain for those values.

PARENTING

"Don't fence him in and he will be all right." Unconditional love does not imply unconditional approval. Symbols and rituals matter: A wooden sword provides confidence and authority; meetings of the Round Table provide structure; making rules before the game is played ensures fair play. Demonstration of charity teaches value. Respect is taught by respecting others even when it is hard to find something respectable about the community drunkard. Life is hard, but the kids can handle it when the parents handle it. Don't explain everything and don't try to understand everything.

OLD AGE

You will die from getting old and that will happen sooner if you don't take care of yourself. That's OK, but you should prepare for it. Your memory will linger on, enhanced by the good will of your survivors. I hope someone brings you flowers before your funeral.

DESPAIR
Focus on others and solutions to your own problems will magically appear in a way you could not discover with focus on yourself. Uncle Ralph nearly missed that point as he tied to drown his sorrow like Walter had done. Walter's life took on nobility as he saved Ralph from his own error.

LOVE
I love "love", but I don't know anything about it. I had to include references to love just to acknowledge its mystery. I would solicit feedback from any reader who has figured it out as it seems important. Its absence destroyed Walter. The rest had better experience with this elusive life force. Isn't it strange that the same thing that held the Kingdom of Johnson together is the thing that tore it apart. Camelot has returned to the land of the imagination'

HAPPINESS
It's everywhere as long as you aren't looking for it. Keep on keeping on and it will hunt you down. Look for it and it will flee.

GUILT
We're all guilty. Forgiveness is a wonderful thing to experience and a free gift to give. Give it often and freely so others don't have to carry that burden around with them. The umbrella isn't as important as the guilt it symbolizes.

PRIDE
Do your best, then, STRUT. Others will envy your work if you are proud of it. They still might not hire you as a barber.

BRAVERY

You can't be brave if you are fearless. Fearlessness suggests stupidity. Press on if you need to get the job done even when the outcome is uncertain. Don't do it just because there is a "Double Dog Dare" on the line. That suggests both stupidity and a false pride.

FEAR

Be brave. Be wise. Press on. Avoid foolishness. Don't get too close to the thick brush where dragons might hide. Keep your sword at the ready.

AUTHORITY

Give appropriate respect, not blind acceptance. Authority figures have their own set of flaws. When prudent disregard for authority is exercised, be ready to accept the consequences. They're not all idiots, but some of them are. Blackie had to go because he embarrassed the preacher.

DEATH

"You're not dead until you are dead. Fight back. Sir Lancelot would be dead in a wastebasket if he just gave up. He didn't even get a notch on his sword for this most important victory. He beat death itself. His victory over the Snow Monster did get him a notch on his sword, but that's just because he needed help getting chiseled loose from the ice.

INTRODUCTION

Carl Johnson here. You will notice a spectacular sword hanging over my bedroom door. The notches on that sword were carved by Merlin commemorating fierce battles and dangerous adventures from my days as Sir Lancelot, Protector of the Kingdom of Johnson. The sword is now retired since my days of knighthood ended when the Kingdom of Johnson was destroyed by the very thing that brought it into existence – **LOVE**.

I will share a few tales of adventures experienced during my days as Sir Lancelot. I am now six years old and have a lot to tell about the last couple of years. My uncle, Ralph Johnson, and his four children, Jane, Dennis, Amy and Kenny, are living on the farm with us. They came to live with us three years ago shortly after their mom (Aunt Sally) died giving birth to Kenny. Uncle Ralph and Dad are brothers. Mom and Dad and my two brothers, Marvin and Lyle make up the entire citizenry of the Kingdom of Johnson. The Kingdom was known simply as the Johnson farm until I redefined our situation. Dad, John Johnson, and Mom, Eunice Johnson, love books and music and, most of all, the people I just named.

Mom reads to us every day from the King James Bible. She says, "We can get to know God by reading about Him." She says "Children's Bible stories are OK, but they make the real stuff God talks about seem like fairy tales." Dad and Uncle Ralph read to us from their favorite books which include Shakespeare and Milton and Keats and Tennyson and Mark Twain and lots of other guys who write really fancy stuff. We are allowed to ask questions when the big words confuse us. We spend a lot of time in the winter reading and make some time for reading even when it is time to plant, cultivate, or harvest crops. Uncle Ralph read a bunch of exciting tales about Kings and Knights and Magicians and Dragons. I immediately knew that my calling was to be a Brave Knight.

I said "Uncle Ralph, these tales of Kings and Knights and Queens are just like living here on the Johnson farm. Mom and Dad are just like a king and Queen. I can be brave and powerful and guard the farm from dangers like dragons and wild beasts. I will henceforth be known as **SIR LANCELOT**."

Uncle Ralph said, "I have been hiding my secret identity until this moment. I am the magician, **MERLIN**. I will cast a spell that protects you from harm when you fight dragons and wild beasts and protect the **KINGDOM OF JOHNSON** from danger."

The very next day, Merlin, brought me a wooden sword. He is wearing a cone shaped hat with a moon and some stars on it and has a stick with a tennis ball on the top that is his magic scepter proving his identity. He cast a spell that protects me from all harm as I perform my duties defending the Kingdom of Johnson from danger. He said, "I will carve a notch on this sword every time you conquer a dangerous foe. We will gather at the **ROUND TABLE** whenever there is an adventure to be told. Tonight you can tell about the first dragon you defeated."

Merlin prepared crowns to be worn by **KING ARTHUR** and **GUINEVERE** at state occasions. He also assembled appropriate royal garments for the king and Queen. We talk about possible names for my brothers and cousins, but Marvin immediately rejects the title of SIR **GALAHEAD.** I solved the entire problem in one fell swoop. "They can all be my **ARMOR BEARERS** so I will have assistance when I need it during a dangerous adventure." This also eliminated memorizing a bunch of hard names and jostling for positions of importance at the Round Table.

The Round Table is an oak dining room table when leaves turn it into an oval table, but it is undeniably a "round table" when the leaves are taken out for our meetings where great adventures are recounted. King Arthur and Guinevere are such humble rulers that they seldom wear their royal crowns and robes even at state events like meetings of the Round Table. Merlin never attends a state event without his magic scepter and magician's hat. One never knows when magic spells will be needed. I always bring the great notched sword.

The armor bearers confirm my accounts and add embellishments to my stories of adventure and daring at the round table. No one is corrected even if some of the details contradict each other. Some of the enhancements are made up on the spot just to allow the teller a chance to participate. Why would anyone complain if the story gets better?

SIR LANCELOT TAKES A NAP

Being Sir Lancelot is a noble calling, One I take very seriously. Five is much too old for such a one as Sir Lancelot to be taking naps unless resting after a long battle. Guinevere has King Arthur's full authority. It is her opinion that Sir Lancelot should take a nap after lunch just like his younger cousins who need the rest so they can serve as effective armor bearers.

She explains "You can serve as a good example by taking your nap without protest in order to benefit those who actually need a nap."

The logic is flawed. Sir Lancelot has a Kingdom to protect with or without armor bearers. Disobeying the Queen might be seen as disobedience to the King, and we all know how that would be viewed. Having never heard the King's views on naps, I go along with the Queen's nap orders, though I feel Merlin's wise advice regarding the responsibility for guarding the Kingdom is closer to Sir Lancelot's proper duty.

I ponder this dilemma as we march up the stairs after lunch, leading a parade of four armor bearers who actually need naps. Sir Lancelot is needed elsewhere. I had planned to go to the barnyard where a new calf arrived just two days earlier. This calf is easy prey for a lion or bear or wolf. Sir Lancelot is needed to risk his life once again in service to the Kingdom. I have never slain a bear or wolf and am wondering what special tactics and dangers will be involved. Dragons are easy, but the lions are fierce competitors. Danger to the new calf seems more eminent with each step up the stairs. I count the steps as I climb the stairs. One, two, three, four, five, six, ...I skip one and then start over. I can't remember seven. That's a tough number to remember. I can go all the way to eleven if someone reminds me of seven. The wolf threat is distracting me! Wolves will be Sir Lancelot's next foe.

I'm in luck. Guinevere didn't think to disarm me prior to the planned nap. I had prepared an elaborate defense for my need of the sword during nap time. It was wasted effort as Guinevere never mentions the sword as she tucks me into bed with two of my armor bearers. I pull the covers over my head, but the queen pulls them down enough to kiss me on the cheek before leaving the room. That's really embarrassing to a full fledged Knight of the Round Table, but it makes me feel good anyway. Like I said, the armor bearers need the nap and are asleep minutes after the bedroom door closes. Sir Lancelot's duty is fulfilled since the armor bearers have his good example to dream about. Now, how to save the calf from the wolves. Wolves! Not merely wolf! That's what will really make this adventure exciting and dangerous. Up 'til now it was always one foe at a time. The story will be better tonight at the Round Table than any previous time. Merlin will be amazed!

Getting out of bed and putting shoes on is easy. You don't have to strip down to skivvies for a nap. Just shoes off and crawl in with your overalls and shirt still on. Even a Knight can be puzzled when blocked from his clear duty. I can't risk going down the stairs, as discovery will defeat the mission and possibly invoke displeasure from the King and Queen. They aren't as enamored with Sir Lancelot's duty to protect the kingdom as Merlin, and might mistake my actions as some sort of disloyalty. A long look out of the upstairs window reveals the danger Sir Lancelot must avert. Sir Lancelot can't stand to watch a tragedy unfold across the yard and down by the barn. The wolves might be sneaking up behind the barn even now. Merlin and King Arthur are on the other side of the kingdom planting corn. The new calf is lying on straw next to the barn and mom cow is licking his fur. Something must be done.

The window is heavy but it is open a bit with a book holding it up. I am able to squeeze through and am soon on the porch roof high above the ground. My sword is thrown to the ground. I am committed. I slip over the edge of the porch roof, hanging onto the gutter. I get a firm grip on the downspout and let go of the gutter. The downspout wasn't built as playground climbing equipment. It breaks loose from the gutter and house and Sir Lancelot swings away from the porch in a great arc still holding onto the downspout. With a mighty clatter the downspout and its rider land in the great lilac bush at the corner of the house. I lie perfectly still several moments. To my surprise, I am unhurt. Merlin's spell really works. Sir Lancelot cannot be harmed. Even more surprising, no one heard the racket and I am undiscovered. It is easy to collect my sword and head for the barnyard where my services are needed.

Merlin comes in from the field for more seed corn and discovers Sir Lancelot asleep on the straw resting his head on the new calf. Mom cow is watching over them both. Sir Lancelot's trusty sword is lying across his chest at the ready. Remember that even a Knight might need a nap after a fierce battle. Merlin lets me get the rest I need. The Round Table is the best ever that evening. King, Queen, Magician all in royal regalia. Sir Lancelot displays the mighty sword with four – that's right – four new notches. A whole pack of wolves! Merlin's spells are proven as they not only protected Sir Lancelot in his greatest adventure, they actually empower flight when required by solemn duty.

    It was a restful nap.

A KNIGHT'S FUNERAL

Sir Lancelot and his entire band of armor bearers find themselves imprisoned by the queen. An evil magician must have cast a spell on her. The prison encloses a rectangle of sand five feet wide by ten feet long. A pail of old kitchen utensils and a few dented pots is present within the prison walls. The armor bearers say the sentence is short and they expect to be liberated when Merlin and King Arthur return from their corn planting work at suppertime.

The very thought of imprisonment is abhorrent to the only fully qualified knight in the Kingdom. Sir Lancelot has a solemn duty to protect the Kingdom. I must escape.

The armor bearers are content to explore the contents of the pail left for their amusement or distraction. They divide up the utensils and pots with a minimum of argument. Everyone wants a pot and the biggest spoon as they are useful for excavation work. Sir Lancelot quietly watches as they plumb the depth of the sand which turns out to be nearly eighteen inches deep. The earth is hard and dry beneath the sand. A pile of sand is created by this effort, giving me a great idea for escape. We can pile the sand so high we can walk right out of our prison. A full hour of digging and piling sand results in a pile no higher than three feet at its peak and that is reduced by a foot when an escapee climbs upon the man made mountain. The chicken wire walls soar to a height of eight feet.

11

Sir Lancelot gazes at his trusty sword with many notches in its handle, each symbolizing victory over a dangerous beast. Many dragons, two lions and four wolves were dispatched, each earning another notch on the handle of his mighty sword. How can an imprisoned and disarmed knight perform his duty as protector of man and beast within the Kingdom? He must guard against the malefactors set on death and destruction to the peaceful inhabitants of the Kingdom of Johnson. My sword is lying on the ground outside the prison walls, well out of reach of the prisoners. I am defeated in my first escape plan, but defeat is not my style. I notice that the excavation required by mountain building comes near to the enclosing fence.

Sir Lancelot must take charge. I commandeer the largest spoon and a table knife. I begin to loosen the hard earth with the knife and scoop it out with the spoon. The equipment can't handle the job. The spoon bends under the strain and no other tool is adequate to create the planned tunnel. A long discussion reveals that the armor bearers are having fun creating roads through the sand and placing sand houses along their route. They have lost any interest in escape plans.

I sit in a corner where I study my prison. Six tall posts create support for the chicken wire walls. A board is nailed between two posts with an entry gate hinged under that board. The gate is secured by a board that reaches between the posts. The board is wedged tightly into a slot on each post. The clever engineering is the work of King Arthur and Merlin. They must have planned to hold dangerous beasts within these walls. No attempt to open the gate from within is feasible. Only giants such as Merlin and Arthur can operate the mechanism of that gate. Earlier attempts by the prisoners to push the gate open revealed the strength of its design.

Sir Lancelot can surely escape this secure prison. I turn my attention to the chicken wire itself. The prisoners had their shoes removed prior to their incarceration. The loops in the wire can be grasped by small hands intent on climbing, but feet are too wide to insert in the wire loops. It would be painful to insert only toes in the wire loops and then rest the climber's weight on the wire in an attempt to climb out of the prison. Toes might actually be severed in such an effort. Unfortunately, none of the armor bearers is willing to see if he can climb on the fence. Sir Lancelot, remembers the spell cast by Merlin, and realizes that he cannot be harmed during his exploits of valor. I began my perilous ascent in the corner where the wire is most stable. Each careful placement of hands and toes in the wire brings me nearer the top of the enclosure. Pulling hard with my hands reduces the pain in my toes as I climb. I protect my hands by wrapping them in my shirt which I pulled off for that purpose.

Thoughts of the king who had offered half his kingdom for a horse when he was trapped ran through my head. I would have traded great value for socks to protect my feet during the climb. But there was no one to trade anything for socks and I have nothing to trade. At the top of the Fence I rest on my stomach on top of the supporting pole. A fall from this great height could be fatal for Sir Lancelot.

Lying on my stomach on top of an eight foot pole is an opportunity for great philosophical thought. It would be just as dangerous to descend back into the prison on one side as it would be to descend to freedom on the other – no hard decision there. I might be killed in either descent. I imagine the great ceremony which will surround Sir Lancelot's funeral. I hope to be buried with my great sword. I am sure there will be a full recounting of my exploits at the funeral. How can anyone but me actually describe all of Sir Lancelot's exploits? Will the King and Queen realize I had sacrificed myself in an attempt to protect the kingdom? Merlin will be inconsolable. I feel hot tears on my cheek as I contemplate death.

Then I remember. Of course! Merlin's spell guarantees Sir Lancelot's protection while performing feats of valor and daring. This escape surely is right up there with Dragon slaying. The shirt is re-wrapped around my hands, and I descend the outside of the sand box prison without incident. I immediately secure the sword with many notches and march triumphantly to the prison walls where I address the armor bearers. I assure them that Sir Lancelot is in charge of the situation and will guarantee their safety and eventual release. Meanwhile, I will seek out adventure which can be recounted at a meeting of the Round Table after supper.

The day is wearing on and no adventure presents itself. It really feels good to have shoes on my sore feet although I usually prefer to go barefooted. Newly shod, I pull the red Radio Flyer chariot near the prison walls. I sit in the wagon outside the prison walls and spend spent a great deal of time instructing the armor bearers on the part each must play in Sir Lancelot's funeral. I never considered writing a will or planning a funeral until my epiphany on top of the prison wall pole. Exhausted by

14

the escape effort and meticulous planning of a state funeral, I stretch out under the oak tree and fall asleep.

Merlin arrives at the prison to free all the prisoners for supper. He is puzzled to find Sir Lancelot asleep under the oak tree while the other prisoners are all found within the prison compound. He says "Sir Lancelot, do you have any reports of great deeds requiring the carving of more notches on the great notched sword?"

The situation clearly demands a story of some sort to explain Sir Lancelot's presence outside the prison walls.

I answer, " The armor bearers can describe the day's events at the Round Table tonight, and I will complete the evening by explaining the details of my funeral. "

Merlin's response is a puzzled look.

LOST

Sir Lancelot and the armor bearers are commanded by King Arthur, himself, to check the woods beyond the pasture for two missing heifers. The fence was damaged yesterday at the back end of the pasture, and the entire herd of milk cows and their offspring decided to test a well known theory: "The grass is always greener on the other side of the fence."

This old saw has clear evidence to prove its truth. The cows can only poke their heads a couple of feet through the fence and the untouched grass just beyond that range is obviously more luxuriant than the well-grazed grass within the confines of the pasture.

King Arthur speculates that the cows knocked down a weak section of the fence as they attempted to reach further into the untouched grass just out of their reach.

Only Sir Lancelot knows the truth. There are dragon tracks near the breached fence. True, the tracks are hard to discern since an entire herd of cows has trampled on them in an attempt to reach greener pastures, but I see them nonetheless. I surmise that a great flying dragon, breathing fire from its nostrils, landed in the pasture intent on destruction and mayhem. When the dragon realized it was in a Kingdom with a Knight of the Round Table present, it took off like its tail was on fire, knocking down the rotten fence post and flattening fifty feet of pasture fence. A dead tree just beyond the damaged fence section is clear evidence of the destruction caused by dragon breath.

Milk cows return to the barn at milking time as milk cows are want to do. A scoop of tasty grain and udders relieved of the milk burden they have been manufacturing during the days grazing is always enough to bring them in. Cows aren't particularly contemplative creatures in spite of the contented appearance they have as they lie around chewing their cud after grazing until their sides poke out like the belly of an old drunk. They just go to the barn at milking time because that is their habit and no other reason is needed.

Young heifers get no scoop of grain and no swollen udders are present requiring relief from the load of milk. They haven't been around long enough to have any established habits. There is no reason for them to leave the lush grazing to return to the barn. As one would suspect, they decided to explore the unfenced woodland for succulent grazing rather than follow the dull routine of the milk cows.

As soon as milking is finished, King Arthur and Merlin replac the broken fence post with a new strong post coated with creosote so it can't rot within two men's lifetimes. They reattach the downed section of fence wire, blocking cows in and heifers out. Now the heifers can't return to the pasture even if they want to.

A complex plan is fashioned to return the two missing heifers. Tomorrow, the kids (oops), armor bearers and Sir Lancelot will find the heifers and drive them down the lane alongside the pasture fence. When they approach, Guinevere will open the gate to the pasture allowing the heifers into the pasture, returning the Kingdom to a state of homeostasis. "A place for everything, and everything in its place". That is the mantra of the Queen. Sir Lancelot realizes that the mission is much more urgent than simply getting things back in place. The heifers are in mortal danger! A dragon is on the loose!

The search party leaves on the rescue and recovery mission just after breakfast the next morning. They cross the pasture to the repaired fence section. Sir Lancelot must be on alert. I scour the ground for dragon tracks and find several which are partially obscured by hoof prints and not a few green cow pies. Give a herd of cattle lots of fresh green grass and you get really moist cow pies. Sir Lancelot long ago learned that it is unwise to kick a cow pie on a hot day. One armor bearer stretches apart the strands of barbed wire midway between fence posts, and all slip through. The armor bearers see the heifers resting in tall grass several hundred feet away.

Sir Lancelot summons his loyal helpers for a planning session. We sit in a circle so everyone can participate. As at the Round table, all are important in a circle. No one is at the head of the table or at its foot. King Arthur explained this philosophy at the first meeting of the Knights of the Round Table. That doesn't suggest there are no leaders. King Arthur is clearly the leader closely followed by the Queen. Merlin might be found anywhere in the circle, but his importance is obvious. All look to Merlin when a question of protocol arises. Today, I hold the stick which is used to draw the plans. I place a rock in the center of the circle, stating "This is the location of the heifers". I scratch a line in the dirt representing the repaired fence line. I then draw two wide circles around to a point behind the heifers to represent the paths two groups will take to position themselves behind the animals so the beasts can be driven down the lane beside the pasture and to the gate. Guinevere will open the gate to allow the heifers back into the pasture from which they escaped.

King Arthur and Merlin are far off planting crops and doing other important mysterious things to keep the Kingdom functioning. It is gratifying to know this most important of all tasks is delegated to the trusty group assembled in the circle. We all take our jobs seriously. I have them count off – "one, two, one, two, one, two." Seven are present so I take no number to maintain balance in the plan. Group one will circle behind the heifers from the right and group two will follow the opposite path. A signal will be given to advance toward the heifers when all are in position.

As protocol dictates, Sir Lancelot designs the signal. Group one will shout, "HE." when in position. Group two will respond with, "HAW" when they are ready. We practice our signals. Calls of "HE – HAW – HE – HAW – HE – HAW" are made until we are all rolling on our backs in fits of laughter as the humor of the thing overcomes us. When order is finally restored, the armor bearers ask, "What is Sir Lancelot's role in the cattle drive is to be?" I stand up with the notched sword held high and announce, " I will protect the entire group from the dragon who started this whole mess". None of the others were aware of the danger involved in our rescue mission until now. I point out the partially obscured dragon tracks and the tree scorched by dragon breath. I nearly frighten my entire entourage back to the castle with my intense description of the danger we face.

A great deal of persuasion is required to get the two groups to execute the elaborate plan arrived at moments earlier. Merlin's spell protecting Sir Lancelot during his exploits is determined to cover all participants in this particular adventure. Besides, if one chickens out and runs to the castle out of fear, he will not be a participant and will thus be unprotected by Merlin's spell which has been proven effective many times by Sir Lancelot. No one wants to be on his own, unprotected in dragon territory.

I leave the council circle stating "I will procede towards the woods, checking for dragon signs and drive off any marauding dragons".

The Heifers stare at the group of kids with curiosity rather than fear. The laughter had first startled them, but they soon go back to absorbing the warm sunlight on their backs and thinking heifer thoughts again. They are in no way alarmed when the teams of cattle drivers move out as planned. I am past the heifer's location, scouting out the thick brush at the edge of the woods. Dragon sign is found everywhere. I am startled at the first loud "HE" from group one. It is followed by a loud "HAW" from group two. Then it begins again. "HE – HAW - HE – HAW" until every member of each group is again flat on his back in fits of laughter. The heifers decide to get up and mosey on toward the pasture, following the fence until it funnels them into the lane and the awaiting gate. The drivers chatter and laugh as they follow the cattle home, glad to be leaving dragon country behind, even though being protected by Merlin's spell and my protective scouting. Guinevere sees the group arriving from the kitchen window and hurries to open the gate.

She congratulates the cattle drivers on their success and then asks "Where is Sir Lancelot?"

Sir Lancelot is missing from the group which headed out two hours earlier to find the lost heifers. An awful silence falls on the cattle drivers as the question sinks in. The last time anyone saw Sir Lancelot he was scouting the edge of a dense forest housing at least one dragon and possibly a large number of them. They begin to shed large tears which the queen has trouble stopping. She suggests they should form a search party to find Sir Lancelot, but none of them agree to go with her. One dead subject is enough for any day in this Kingdom. Guinevere knows it is her duty to protect the group in front of her rather than abandon them in a search of the missing Knight who is probably in no danger anyway. She is curious as to what makes them so reluctant to return to the field from which they had just come.

Meanwhile, I decide to explore the forest. I trust Merlin's protective spell. I'm not even sure the tracks I see are real dragon tracks as I have never tracked a real dragon before. I do find a lot of broken branches which could have been broken by a passing dragon. I am convinced the dead tree was scorched by dragon breath. There is enough evidence to make a Knight cautious, but not so much that he is afraid to proceed. I weave a crooked course trying to stay away from the thickest underbrush so I won't accidentally stumble on a waiting dragon. I top a small rise in the ground and see a small pond below. Surely there will be dragon footprints in the soft ground near the pond. I will see their exact shape so

I will never again be uncertain when I see a fresh dragon footprint.

I stand on the high ground a long time and survey every inch of the surrounding woods. No dragon is present. I carefully make my way to the pond; often turning quickly to be sure no dragon is attempting to sneak up on me. At one point I am sure I feel hot dragon breath on the back of my neck. This will not do. Sir Lancelot is ever aware. I dive to the ground and roll onto my back with my sword at the ready, but it is a false alarm. Courage is not fearlessness. It is performance in the face of danger. Merlin himself has clarified that point. Sir Lancelot will never be embarrassed by fear. The fear is proof of his courage. It is impossible to have courage with no fear.

I watch a dozen turtles slip off rocks into the water as I approach. I make my way entirely around the pond several times but find no dragon tracks. My own tracks are the only evidence of visits to the pond. The sun is high in the sky. I am tired from my continuous state of high alert. I stretch out on a soft grassy spot and plan to rest only a few minutes.

I am startled awake by an angry squirrel chattering in protest over my presence from a branch in the tree above me. I notice the sun is lower in the sky. I also notice a grumbling in my stomach. I am hungry. This adventure started just after breakfast and lunchtime has long since passed. I look about trying to remember my path to the pond. It all looks the same. I remember coming down a small hillside, but the entire pond is surrounded by higher ground. I study my footprints near the pond but they give no clue as to the direction from which I had come. I remember that the sun was behind me as I approached the pond.

That remembered, I set out toward the sun, forgetting that it had moved in the sky since my arrival. Nothing familiar is seen as I top the small hill. I continue toward the sun, continuously scanning the horizon for any familiar sight. None appears. I begin to walk more quickly, forgetting my fear of stumbling onto a dragon. The sun is getting lower and lower in the sky and I am really getting worried. I am sure I didn't come this far earlier because I was proceeding slowly and cautiously during my entire penetration of the forest. Now, I am walking fast, even running a few steps at times. This forest might be magic, growing larger as I try to escape.

At last a clearing appears ahead as I top a small rise in the ground. I run toward the clearing, certain I will see the castle and its surrounding buildings, most notably the large red barn and the tall silo next to it. Relief is palpable as I break into the clearing and spot the large red barn with its attendant tall silo. It is a surprisingly long way off, but my steps are light as I alternately walk and run toward the buildings. I realize I was truly in a magical forest as I approach the buildings. The Kingdom has been rearranged. The machinery shed is gone. The house which had been sitting on higher ground than the barn is now on level ground nearer the barn. Where is the old McCormic-Deering tractor which sits near the barn since it quit running long before I arrived in the Kingdom? I cautiously approach the unfamiliar house.

Now I am really frightened! This isn't the place I left this morning! A beautiful lady in a blue frock with an apron around her waist opens the door and looks at the youngster standing on her porch with great tears in his eyes. She wipes flour from her hands onto the apron and hugs me tightly. She exclaims, "You must be one of the Johnson boys. Your family is the only one around here with such light blonde hair and blue eyes. How did you get here? What's this?" She noticed the great notched sword.

I immediately regain my composure as I am reminded of my stature as principle Knight of the Round Table. The lady identifies herself as Mrs. Eriksson.

Certain that I had escaped the magic forest and had been correctly identified, I launch into a description of how I arrived at this place. Mrs. Eriksson steps into the house holding my hand and calls out, "George, we have a visitor!" A kindly old man comes into the kitchen and extends his hand to me as Mrs. Eriksson says "This is Sir Lancelot. He has spent the day in the woods dragon hunting."

Not lacking in social graces, I continue to shake George's hand even as I expound my tale of the Dragon hunt and lost heifers and magic forest. George is laughing as he phones the Johnson house. He asks "are you are missing any Knights?" King Arthur grabs the phone from Guinevere and pumps George with a thousand questions. "Is he all right? Where is he? How did he get to your place?"

The answers are hilarious. George could not answer the questions without laughing so hard he found it difficult to speak. He says "Sir Lancelot is fine. He has been driving dragons out of the Brule Woods. He came over here to chase our dragons away as well. We will be

24

happy to drive Sir Lancelot home for the service he has provided."

King Arthur responds with "You and Mrs. Eriksson are invited to supper at the castle and a meeting of the Round Table to follow." George accepts the cryptic invitation. The Erikssons live two miles from the Johnson farm as the crow flies and three miles by road. Nourished by two cookies and a glass of milk, I am on my way home within a short time seated in the front seat of their pickup between George and Mrs. Ericksson.

We arrive at the Johnson castle shortly where a great celebration takes place. After supper, the Erickssons are assigned special places at the Round Table, what with their being neighboring royalty. Merlin has two spare crowns which he places on their heads. All participants wear their royal garb. This adventure tale tops the list. A dragon is chased through a magic forest until the frightened beast promises never to return to either the Johnson or Eriksson kingdoms ever again. FOREVER!

George thanks Sir Lancelot for his brave service in ridding the country of the dragon. An alliance between the two kingdoms is forged which exists to this very day.

FROZEN KNIGHT

Northern Wisconsin winters get really cold. The temperature stayed below freezing the entire month of January. Merlin says that makes candles last longer because the wax can't melt. One morning it is nearly thirty degrees below zero. When the men come in for breakfast after milking, the scarves around their necks are covered with frost from their breath. The cows are kept in the barn and fed hay and grain instead of grazing. Cows put out a lot of body heat. The barn is always warm because clear plastic tarp seals all the broken windows and cracks around doors excepting those used for entrance and egress.

The infrared lights stay on in the chicken house, and it is also sealed tightly with bales of straw stacked around the perimeter to keep drafts from working up through the cracks in the rough floor. The floor itself is pretty well sealed by several inches of chicken manure and old straw kicked out of the nests. The house has storm windows attached and rags stuffed under all the doors except the kitchen door which is the only one used during cold weather. It is as warm in as cold out.

Winter days are short and the long days of planting, cultivating and harvesting crops are over for the season. The kids like winter because the adults are not as busy. Reading, storytelling, and singing fill the evenings. We have two steers hanging in the larder and at least ten hams curing in the smokehouse with big slabs of bacon stored in parchment paper covered with salt. The basement shelves are filled with canned goods in Mason Jars.

Nearly any food can be canned. It often tastes better than fresh food because the spices and other ingredients have time to penetrate every morsel. I especially like the fish balls which are a Swedish traditional food. I am also fond of jam made from strawberries, blueberries, gooseberries and choke cherries. Other treats like rhubarb and apple sauce are added to baked items to form pies and dumplings and lots of other deserts. More attention is paid to complex recipes when more time is available to the cook.

Our winter stores overflow. The potato bin in the basement is piled high. The preacher often drops by for supper and spends the night so he can share the hearty breakfast which is served as soon as milking is over. He never goes to the barn to help with chores like other visitors. Mom says he has a lot of allergies. He has a great low voice and plays the guitar and knows more songs than anyone. Mom says singing for your supper is an old tradition.

I've got to tell you about those fish balls! Every spring we spread a net across the mouth of the creek when the red horse suckers are spawning and the whole community works for a week cleaning huge tubs full of the fish which most of the world considers inedible. After they are cleaned and skinned, they are ground up, bones and all, like hamburger. The fish is then mixed with a little raw sausage and seasoned with salt and pepper. This mixture is made into balls the size of golf balls. They are packed in quart jars. The jars are then nearly filled with water and an onion is placed in each one. They are boiled until the fish balls are solid and a layer of fat is floating on the top of each jar. The lids are screwed on the jars while they are still hot. If you do it right, the lid is sucked down sealing the jar as it cools, preserving the fish balls for as long as you can keep people from eating them. They are served on mashed potatoes with gravy and corn or peas or green beans. Ham, chicken, and roast beef are usually reserved for Sunday dinner, but fish balls at supper and bacon at breakfast turn up most any time.

Mom brags about having fresh vegetables and produce in the summer, but the best eating is done in the winter when it is too cold to do much else. Dad says that an able bodied man's first duty is to feed his family. No one would dare accuse King Arthur of failing in that regard. The preacher doesn't feed anyone but himself. He told dad that his first duty should be to spread the gospel. Dad says he would like to agree with him, but then they would both be wrong. I think it is a joke because everyone laughs. I don't get it. When adults sit around chewing the fat, a lot of things are said that make no sense. When I describe my adventures, everyone can follow the logic with very little explanation.

Now I remember, I started to tell you about that really cold morning. Uncle Ralph says he will show us some magic. Merlin puts on his coat and barn cap and then he puts on Merlin's cone-shaped hat with the moon and stars on it over his barn hat. We all go out with just coats on so we can see the magic. We have no plan to stay out long in this cold. Merlin stands on the edge of the porch which is a concrete platform several feet higher than the ground. He holds his magic scepter with the gold knob on it out over the snow bank. He makes some spit and leans his head back. He spits in a great arc. When the spittle hits the snow, it doesn't 'sink in like we expect. It crackles, freezing solid as it hits the cold snow and bounces along the surface. He does the same thing twice more with the same amazing result. He says, "That's really cold!" We all try it with less success. Merlin shows us the secret. You have to spit up to let the spit get really cold before it hits the snow. I get a spit ball to crackle and freeze after a couple of tries. No one else gets their spit to freeze. Merlin says "You might have some magician in you as well as valor." I think I will get him to make me a scepter so I can practice magic.

We all go back in the house to get warm and discuss the physics of super cooled liquids and crystal formation and other stuff I still don't comprehend. King Arthur and Merlin and two men from the co-op get dressed in their warmest winter clothes for ice harvesting. They say, "You have to make hay when the sun is shining." They say, "When life gives you lemons, you should make lemonade." I guess that means "When it is too cold to tend crops, you collect ice."

The men take the tractor with a sleigh out onto the lake ice. They have a big area where they shoveled all the snow off last week. They take saws with great teeth and saw out blocks of ice. The blocks are so heavy they have to be lifted with a block and tackle pulley system. Ice tongs grip the blocks of ice and are used to slide them into place on the big sleigh. When the sleigh is loaded with two layers of huge ice blocks, it is dragged by the tractor to the ice house where it is unloaded. The ice is stacked in layers separated by an inch of sawdust from the sawdust pile at the saw mill.

My grandfather built the Ice house many years ago to store ice which is sold in summer time to keep ice boxes cold for storing milk and meat. If you put salt on the ice it will get so cold you can make ice cream on a hot summer day. It is really hard work turning the crank on the ice cream maker, but the ice cream is so good it is worth the effort.

My grandfather was a real innovator. He dug a ditch from the ice house to the basement of the house and covered a large pipe with dirt. When it gets real hot in July he turns on a fan in the pipe to blow cold air into the house. We don't use the cold air unless it is really hot because it melts some of the ice we sell for ice boxes.

Mom dresses me and the armor bearers in many layers of clothes covered by rubber boots, coats, scarves, stocking hats and mittens. We are preparing to go to the lake to watch the men harvest ice. The layers of clothes are so bulky you have to walk stiff legged and your arms won't come all the way down to your side. Even with all those clothes, your nose nearly freezes unless you wrap your scarf so high that only your eyes are visible. We head outside toward the lake across the road. We flop onto our backs and try to wave our arms to create snow angels. It is so cold that the snow has a hard crust on it and we can't make good angels. I am glad I'm not dressed in metal armor like a real knight. I'll bet that metal would be pretty cold in this weather. Your tongue would stick to it if you licked it. I once licked the pump handle in cold weather and my tongue stuck to it. Mom had to pour a whole pail of water on my face to get me free without tearing my tongue out of my mouth. I still got a sore spot where I tried to pull it loose at first.

The men leave for the ice house to unload the ice and warn us to stay away from the area where they are harvesting ice so we won't fall in. We get tired of pretend skating because our boots don't slide well on the ice. We throw snow at each other but it doesn't work well because it is too cold to pack good snowballs and our many layers of clothing prevent a good throw. I notice there is open water where the creek enters the lake. It seems odd that the ice can be so thick out here in the middle and not freeze near the creek. The temperature should be the same over there.

I decide to see if I can figure out this odd pattern of freezing and head for the mouth of the creek. As I near the mouth of the creek, I can tell the ice isn't as thick. It doesn't crack so I feel safe, but it does seem to sink down a bit under my weight.

Suddenly, the ice gives way and I plunge under water. Cold water! I can't swim! My many layers of clothing cause me to bob up in the water like a cork. The water can't penetrate all these clothes, so I'm not cold except for my soaked mittens and face. I paddle frantically for the edge of the ice and try to pull myself out. I can't get a grip and the ice breaks off. I paddle back to the edge and try again. Over and over I keep falling back as the edge of the ice breaks. The armor bearers see what is happening and run toward me. I warn them that they will fall in if they get near me. They run to get help at the ice house and at the house.

Mom Grabs her coat and runs toward the lake with no boots on. She is really cold and really scared. Meanwhile, I finally manage to crawl up on the ice and crawl a long way toward the thick ice. I am exhausted from the desperate effort to escape a watery grave and roll onto my back to rest. My water soaked clothes begin to freeze and the insulation of my ice cocoon helps me to maintain my body temperature. I really am not very wet because I wasn't in the water long enough to have water soak through all the clothing layers. My fingers are stinging because my wet mittens didn't keep them warm. My face and nose hurt from the cold. I attempt to raise my arm to put my hands inside my coat and discover I am entombed in an icy coat of armor which is frozen to the lake ice. I can't move.

Mom is running across the lake with her unbuttoned coat flying behind her. She is calling my name, but I can't answer because my teeth are chattering so badly. I can't move. Mom is afraid I'm dead until she gets close enough to see my eyes are moving and my teeth are chattering and tears of relief are streaming from my eyes. She's crying too. She is probably colder than I am. She bends forward to pick me up but is amazed that she can't move me. I am frozen to the lake ice. The men are now running toward me. I imagine they will have to saw out a huge block of ice with me attached and load my ice block on the sleigh to take me to the house where my icy armor suit can be melted.

I am really stuck to the ice. It takes a trip to the ice harvesting site to get two flat bladed ice axes used to shave ice blocks into shape. I am finally chiseled free of the ice, but I'm frozen spread eagled with no way to move. Mom runs ahead of Merlin and King Arthur who are carrying me to the house. She has the bathtub half full of warm water by the time we arrive. A bucket of warm water melts the ice at my arms to let my arms move enough to submerge all but my head in the warm water. I'm starting to get feeling in my hands. They really hurt from the cold. In a few minutes my soaked clothing is all removed, and I am rapidly warming up. I am toweled dry with warm towels heated in the oven during the thawing process. I stand on a heat register with a blanket around me describing my recent adventure.

I explain "I saw a gigantic snow monster sneaking up on us. I chased it all the way to the open water where it fell in and melted. I didn't even have the notched sword with me but the terrified monster fled anyway. He melted when he hit the water, but I was running so fast that I slid right into the open water behind him. I swam back to the ice and crawled out. I decided to rest until help arrived and got stuck to the ice."

Merlin says he will carve a special big notch on my sword for the vanquished snow monster. Mom is crying as she is laughing about the whole situation. She worries too much.

RIDING LESSONS

Sir Lancelot is a seasoned Knight of the Round Table. Yep, that's me! With encouragement from Merlin and help from six loyal armor bearers, I have slain dragons, lions and wolves. These exploits are enumerated in records kept by Merlin in the Castle. Each exploit has occurred within walking distance of the Castle. I have been careful to hide from Merlin the fact that I have no warhorse from which to battle foes located far from the Castle. I wonder if his protective spell extends beyond the kingdom.

Today, I will learn to ride so I can range far and wide as I destroy fierce beasts, dragons, and the like. There are no horses in the Kingdom. I study horses each time I find opportunity. They are graceful, strong, fast, and tireless. They are really big. Once I saw a Shetland pony. He seemed to have all the features of a warhorse in a compact package. I think I might be able to get on his back if I stand on a chair next to him. I'm not as big as you might think from the great deeds documented in Merlin's records. I have a great sword with many notches in its handle proving my valor. The Olssons have the Shetland pony of which I speak. His name is Sam, a bit undignified for a warhorse, but I could rename him if he were to become my steed.

I believe I must learn to ride if I am to have any chance of the King purchasing a warhorse for me. At church, I asked Jimmy Olsson "How much money do you think your dad would want for Sam?"

Jimmy said, "Fifteen dollars would probably buy Sam since my brother sand I are both afraid to ride him."

I said, "Man! That's a lot of money!" The Olsons have two other horses and a donkey. The donkey would surely be an undignified warhorse. The quarter horses are far too big and would probably cost even more. It seems I should concentrate on Sam if I am ever to get a warhorse. Meanwhile, I am going to become a great rider.

I ask a lot of questions which might tip off others regarding my plans. "How fast can a horse run? What do horses eat? How does one get on a horse? What makes him go where you want? Has King Arthur ever thought about getting a horse? Where could a horse stay in our Kingdom?"

Most answers point out an amazing coincidence. Cows and horses are a lot alike except the cows are slower, and you can't milk horses. They are about the same size. They eat the same stuff. We may not have any horses, but we have a bunch of cows. It might be good for a beginning rider to learn on an animal that is a bit slower anyway. Speed can be considered later. I'll bet you can see how this is unfolding. I'll start my riding lessons on cows and then transition to horses when I am an expert.

I am familiar with each of our cows. The brown Guernsey's are the smallest of the milk cows but they run around a bit faster than the bigger black and white Holsteins, especially if the Holsteins' udders are full of milk. The Black Angus steers are in-between sized, but they'll butt you if you mess with them. The two young heifers are a perfect size but they run around so much that it's hard to get near them.

I study the cow herd with great interest, leaning on the pasture gate for hours at a time. I am planning a daring adventure. I notice that they spend most of the morning after milking grazing in the pasture. This will be a great time to get some practice riding as the cows wander from each bit of forage at a leisurely pace. I know I can not get on top of one of these giant animals while it is standing up. Fortunately, they have a habit of lying down in the afternoon as they chew their cud. When they get back up for evening milking time, they move even slower because their udders are heavy with milk.

I begin walking into the pasture to search for the right cow. King Arthur is pleased with my interest in the cows. They are an essential element to the economic well-being of the Kingdom. King Arthur inquires "Would you like to help with milking?"

I answer, "I am very interested in cows. I can probably learn a lot about them when we are milking." This adds nothing to my scheme, but I go along with the idea to divert attention from my real purpose in getting to know the cows better. I am standing next to Clara, a big Holstein, as Merlin attaches the milking machine to her udder. He begins by cleaning the udder with a rag soaked in warm water. As I watch with great interest, he throws a belt over Clara's back and slings the milking machine under her belly on the belt. Each teat is sucked into a rubber lined cup and the machine sucks all the milk out of the engorged udder. Things are going well until Clara thinks a fly is biting her. She swishes her urine soaked tail at the fly but it wraps around my face instead. It nearly knocks me down.

Merlin laughs and says "Put your head right against the cow's flank when you are attaching milking machines so the tail swat won't wrap around your face like a towel snapping you." I'm learning more than I want to know. I decide right then and there that milking cows will be low on my list of occupation choices. Fighting dragons is more fun than milking cows. Less dangerous, too!

It is clear that I enjoy studying the cows in the pasture more than in the barn. When milking is over, a huge wheelbarrow is filled with manure from the gutter and wheeled out the side door of the barn. It is wheeled along a board on top of the manure pile and dumped. When the pile gets too big, a loader bucket is attached to the tractor and the manure is loaded into a manure spreader so it can be spread on the fields as fertilizer.

Merlin says "There are many hard choices in life. If you are up to your neck in manure and someone throws a shovelful at you – Should you duck?" I don't know the answer even though I may be faced with choices like that many times in the future.

I avoid milking time after the first lesson. I am too small to handle the cleanup job. I can't carry more than a gallon of milk in the milk pail. I can't haul milk from the milking machines to the milk house. Heavy ten gallon milk cans float in a tank of cold water to cool the fresh warm milk. The milk is poured into the cans through a giant strainer funnel from the milk pail. A cloth at the bottom of the strainer is changed often so junk that falls in the milk is strained out before the milk is contaminated. The milk strainer, milk pails and milking machines are cleaned after each milking in stainless steel sinks built for that purpose. I can't pick up the heavy stainless steel strainer and milking machines and put them in the sink for cleaning' I'm mostly in the way when milking is in progress. The whole process takes about two hours every morning and night. The term "milking" includes all of these activities. There are a lot of things harder than slaying dragons and such. The hardest part about milking is realizing that you have to do it all over again twice every day.

After two weeks of studying cow behavior, I am ready to start my riding lessons. I am careful not to have any adults observe my efforts. I am pretty sure it would meet with some sort of disapproval although I see no particular reason for disapproval. I don't ask permission since no rule had been promulgated regarding cow riding, and I don't want to risk an unfavorable ruling on the idea.

I wait until Clara fills her stomach with forage and lies down to chew her cud. Perfect! I walk up to Clara from the side without legs sticking out. I don't want to get tangled up in flailing legs if she decides to get up as I approach. She turns her head to look at me as I climb on her back. She is a really big animal. I am afraid of what might happen when I climb on.

Nothing happens. She just lays there chewing her cud. I lean forward and shout "get up!" Still nothing. Maybe she doesn't hear me. She turns her head toward me and licks my face. I am off balance, leaning forward and can't jerk back fast enough to avoid that rough tongue. It feels like the roughest sandpaper you can find being rubbed across your face. I am defeated. Clara is truly a contented cow. She is content to let me ride her as much as I want, but she isn't about to get up just for my entertainment.

Riding lesson number one is successful in as much as I learned how to mount my steed. I walk back to the house to get a drink of water out of the dipper hanging in the milk pail on the porch. I then head to the sandbox prison where my armor bearers are making sand castles and sit outside the prison walls telling them of my first successful riding lesson. I explain "I will put on a demonstration when I am really good at riding, but the riding lessons are to be kept secret until then." The authorities don't even bother to incarcerate me with the rest of the prisoners in the afternoons as has become the Kingdom's custom. I am always out within a few minutes of the internment anyway, and they decided I might teach the others to escape or I might become injured during my own escapes.

I hear King Arthur and Guinevere discussing the addition of a chicken wire roof over the prison walls to prevent my escape, but Merlin talks them out of it. He says "Sir Lancelot will just find another way out if we enclose the top of the prison." Merlin is my hero. I think his real objective is to preserve my freedom. When my stories become too fanciful and others suggest backing down a bit, Merlin insists that I should not be fenced in. He means it both literally and figuratively."

I will resent and fight limitations placed around me by bureaucrats and authority figures all my life due to Merlin's insightful training. At supper Guinevere asks

"Did you hurt yourself?" My face is red. I can't very well say that Clara licked me, can I? I said "It resulted from a close call from a fire breathing dragon which I poked in the nose just as it attempted to incinerate me with its fiery breath". No one questions that answer from me as my dragon fighting reputation is unequalled. I don't feel like I misled anyone since I didn't request another notch in my sword for this event. (A cow licking doesn't qualify as an adventure.)

I return to the pasture at cud chewing time the next day to continue my training. I decide to give Clara one more try. The mount is again uneventful. This time I have the notched sword and poke her in the side with it. Clara bellows her indignation at the insult and clumsily heaves to her feet. She rolls onto her folded legs and lurches forward as she straightens out her long back legs. This surprising action pitches me forward and I fall to the ground over her head as she stands completely up. She leans down to lick me again and I get my arm up just in time to prevent a second raspy lick on the face. Her tongue catches my shirt sleeve and nearly pulls it into her mouth. I think she wants to eat my shirt.

She follows me to the pasture gate like she thinks I am going to feed her something. It's a real drag when someone insists on being your friend as you try to escape. I describe my second riding lesson to the prisoners in the sandbox with as much enthusiasm as I can muster. I recount, "I mounted my steed but was bucked off." I omit the licking episode. It may be heroic to be eaten by a lion after a valiant fight, but it would be ignominious to be eaten by a cow. This time I pick up a bit of information that makes me decide to ride a Hereford instead of a Holstein. The Herefords have more meat on their bones. When Clara stood up, I was hit in the straddle by a long row of back bones that really hurt.

My third riding lesson begins at cud chewing time the next day. I head for Sally, a white faced Red Hereford with a round meaty spinal column. She is a bit shorter than Clara. A fall from her back during a clumsy dismount might be less dangerous. The cows are so used to me wandering among them by now that Sally ignores me completely until I am on her back. She apparently imagines a mountain lion has leaped upon her. Her frightened reaction is instantaneous. She leaps to her feet and runs straight toward the pasture fence. I grab hold of her hair with both hands and drop the notched sword as we swing into action. I realize we are going to crash right through the fence. I close my eyes and hang on for dear life. I am really going to be in trouble for this one. Sally makes a ninety degree turn just short of the fence at full speed. I make no turn whatever, following the known laws of physics. I hit the fence with a mighty crash and experience first hand why the cows avoid that electric fence wire strung half way up the fence post. Merlin's spell doesn't work since I am just doing riding lessons instead of feats of valor.

I roll quickly away from the bite of the electric fence. Wow! That hurts a lot. My pants and shirt are both torn by the barbed wire and I have several cuts on my arms, legs and trunk that are bleeding. I lay still fearing shattered bones are sticking out all over my body until I realize I am lying in fresh cow pies. I limp to the house for help. Guinevere strips me naked and throws my clothes in the trash can. She scrubs the filth from my body in the bath tub. After the manure is washed from my hair, she drains the tub and fills it with clean water and soaps my wounds clean. I am then made to stand for inspection while mercuricomb antiseptic is applied to each of my wounds. That stuff burns like fire. This is why kids don't show moms their scrapes and abrasions. The injury is bad enough without being punished by the treatment.

I'm sure I gave some lame excuse for my injuries but I don't remember what it was. It's hard for a Knight of the Round Table to maintain his dignity when he is striped naked by a woman who doesn't believe his account of the day's events. I was lucky to avoid being imprisoned with the rest of the subjects for my own safety. I made solemn promises to end my dragon fighting adventures. I never mentioned cow riding so I guess I can return to that activity, but I've lost my taste for riding lessons for the time being.

I think Flying will be a better way to get around anyway.

??!!WHAT'S THAT SMELL!!??

I am becoming a recluse in the middle of a crowd. I attentively guard the Kingdom against interlopers and dangers of every sort. Merlin never lacks interest in my adventure tales, but the rest of the inhabitants of the kingdom are becoming complacent since I have been so effective in warding off danger which might affect them. That's the whole trouble with doing your job exceptionally well. You make it seem easy and no one can appreciate the effort you are expending on their behalf.

I notice that the King and Queen don't wear their royal attire at meetings of the Round Table. Merlin always brings his magic scepter and hat with stars and a moon on it. I never fail to bring the notched sword, but the notches aren't accumulating like they did at first. I can count them reliably now that I've gotten past stumbling at seven. Twenty three notches account for the dispatch of four wolves, two lions, a giant Hawk and sixteen Dragons. We debated about adding a notch for the Dragon I routed from the Magic Woods, but Merlin said it deserved a notch since I forced him to promise never to return.

Now, let's discuss one of the least significant of the barnyard creatures. Chickens. We have lots of chickens. There are so many that we don't even bother to name most of them. An exception to that rule is made for several of the more aggressive roosters. It is a strange reality that the biggest roosters are often the most peaceable and the smaller brightly colored bandy roosters are the most aggressive. The big white roosters have the loudest wake up cock-a-doodle. One bandy rooster is named Adolph because he attacks anything that comes near him. Adolph nearly got killed attacking a car in the driveway. I hardly ever walk around the Kingdom without the notched sword partly because it has saved me from a rooster attack on several occasions. I saved one of my armor bearer's life when Adolph flew at him, knocking him down and scratching at the back of his head with sharp claws and beak. I whacked Adolph with the notched sword and he flew over the fence to escape.

We have Guinea hens as well. They are noisy birds that aren't good for either of the two reasons chickens exist. They produce few eggs and lousy meat. They make a racket when a predator approaches so they are allowed to roost with the chickens and have run off many a fox or weasel intent on a chicken dinner. The queen selects a big hen that isn't laying anymore or one of the younger roosters for Sunday dinner. The roosters are tough and have to be boiled, but some of the hens can be fried for an extra special treat. At least two chickens are cooked if the preacher is coming to dinner.

The laying hens are kept in the chicken house with a long row of boxes filled with straw. They have a yard they can run around in during the daytime where we throw cracked corn and rolled oats for their nourishment. A few of the big roosters are kept in the henhouse, but most of the roosters run about the farm unrestricted. In the henhouse they just eat the hen's feed and don't lay any eggs so they are pretty much useless. King Arthur says the hens won't lay any eggs if we don't leave a few roosters in the henhouse with them. I guess those are pretty tough roosters marching around and commanding the hens to lay eggs. A few hens also run free just because they got out and we can't catch them. One of the queen's chores is to collect eggs from the henhouse every morning. We box some of them up for sale at the co-op store and use the rest for cooking and eating. Eggs are part of nearly everything eaten on the farm.

We kids volunteered to collect eggs. We left some eggs in the nests and broke a bunch more so that job is still part of the Queen's morning chores. We also let quite a few laying hens out to join the free ranging roosters and the previously escaped hens. Fresh eggs, fried potatoes, bacon and lots of milk and coffee are always on the breakfast table. We have raw oats rolled at the feed store to break the husks off and flatten them out. They are cooked as oatmeal for our breakfast and served raw to the chickens for theirs. Fresh baked bread is served at nearly every meal with lots of freshly churned butter. I can eat a whole loaf of hot bread and butter if there is any strawberry jam to spread on it. But, the wonderful smell of breakfast isn't the smell with which we're concerned in this story.

The free ranging chickens build nests anywhere they feel like it. They often appear with a bunch of little yellow chicks following them around. We capture the chicks and put them in a big warm box for a couple of weeks and feed them ground corn until we can tell which ones are roosters. Then we put the pullets into the henhouse and set the roosters free to scratch out their own place in the world. They are always at the greatest risk for Sunday dinner.

We kids are tasked with finding the free ranging chicken nests and collecting those eggs. We have about a dozen nests located in various parts of the barn and machine shed that regularly produce eggs. If we catch a hen sitting on the nest, we tuck its wings under our arm so she can't flap and hold her legs so she can't kick and put her in the henhouse. About half the time the hen gets loose before we get her into the henhouse. Hens are strong birds.

Now for that smell I told you about. We discovered a nest behind some boards in the machine shop. Instead of one or two eggs like we find in the known nests, there are forty or fifty eggs in this hidden nest. I start to load them into the basket with my other eggs found that morning and one of them breaks. The sulfurous smell of a rotten egg is twice as bad as a straight shot from a frightened skunk. We report our find to Merlin who is carrying milk to the milk house. He helps us separate the few rotten eggs from the good eggs we collected earlier. He washes the bad smell of the broken rotten egg off the good eggs and cleans the wire basket we are carrying them in. Merlin says, "Leave the nest of rotten eggs alone as they are useless."

I ponder the terrible waste of forty or fifty eggs. We have discussed the possibility of an egg fight several times in the past. We would never throw rocks at each other even in a mock battle. Someone could get hurt and the resulting punishment would probably hurt even more. Eggs would make perfect missiles and won't cause any injury as they will break on impact. The targets will be marked by the broken egg. We know better than to waste eggs in such a mock battle because waste is prohibited on the farm.

"Waste not, want not!" This is another of the queen's many axioms which guide moral choices on the farm as surely as the Ten Commandments. In fact, these axioms have more impact than the Ten Commandments because I can think of many axioms and only two commandments. One is to go to church every Sunday unless it is really hard, and the other is to not steal. The other eight must not be as important. "A stitch in time saves nine". "Look before you leap." "Let a sleeping dog lie." (go figure – I've never heard a dog tell a lie – especially while sleeping). A lot of grown-up talk really doesn't make sense.

We have ammunition for an egg fight and no waste will occur as they are declared worthless by Merlin himself. We get a cardboard box and line it with straw before we collect the rotten eggs. They are more fragile than regular eggs. The first one we broke really smelled bad. Forty-three eggs cover the bottom of the box when we are finished. I have a great plan. We will divide the armor bearers into two groups which will stand about twenty feet apart. Each group will be given an equal portion of the eggs. I will stand against the barn with my sword held high. When I swing my sword down, the egg fight will commence. We will determine the winning side by the number of eggs striking members of each side.

A problem is noted as the eggs are divided. One team has an extra egg. I announce a new plan. I will take the extra egg and throw it high in the air. When it hits the ground, the egg fight will commence. All of the other rules remain unchanged. This will really be fun!

The two teams get behind their respective lines and I stand between them against the barn so as not to get in the way of the action. I am proud of myself for designing the game in such a way that the armor bearers get all the fun and I serve only as coach. Also, I smelled that first rotten egg and decided that being hit by one of these stink bombs might not be as fun as it first sounds.

All is ready. I launch the signal egg in a high arc. One of my armor bearers shouts "Geronimo!" and throws a rotten egg straight at me before the signal egg even hits the ground. Both teams immediately discharge all forty-two rotten eggs at me and I am bathed head to toe in the most awful stinking mess God has ever created. It wouldn't be half as bad to be buried in manure up to my neck and have someone throw a shovelful at me. I know that if the question is revised to ask of you are buried up to your neck in manure and someone throws a rotten egg at you would you duck? The answer is an easy Yes!

The rascals run to hide in the barn. They don't need to do that. I have no interest in pursuit for some sort of retribution. I am on my knees vomiting breakfast and possibly last night's supper as well.

I sure didn't see that coming.

CRAZY KID

Winters are cold. Snow is deep. Old cars don't run reliably. Tires blow out. Spring roads are full of mud holes. Gasoline is expensive (ten to fourteen cents a gallon). Chores have to be done twice every day, even Sunday. So, church attendance in Superior is necessarily infrequent. Sunday clothes are worn thin and patched partly due to the difficulty of travel.

But, even considering the obstacles, the Johnson Kingdom is known far and wide as a Christian domain. King Arthur, Merlin, the Olsons, the Knudsons, and even crazy Walter Noland got together years ago and built the community church which serves the whole farming community. They had previously driven all the way to Superior (more than twenty five miles) to attend the big Baptist church in town with over two hundred members and a preacher who has a degree from Bethel Theological Seminary in St. Paul, Minnesota.

A convoy of several tractor drawn sleighs and one drawn by a team of horses with three generations of the Olson Family wrapped in heavy robes like everyone else in the convoy attends Christmas Eve service every year at the big church in Superior. There are bags of candy and peanuts and an apple for each child. There is carol singing. There is a play with real sheep, a manger, and a real baby. There is a moment when every member of the congregation holds a lighted candle high above his head and sings Silent Night. No country church can match that grandeur.

The whole farm community assembles the convoy right after the pot luck dinner at the community church the day before Christmas. They sleep in the church basement in Superior after the Christmas Eve service and return home the next day to resume winter chores and await rebirth of the cold wasteland in the coming spring. A skeleton crew of teen age boys attends to the necessary chores on the abandoned farms Christmas Eve and Christmas morning. They are celebrated with special recognition and gift giving around the Christmas trees. Ropes are dragged behind the sleighs and bigger kids can ride on sleds tied to the ropes part of the way. They get everyone cold when they climb under the robes to get warm after a ride on a sled. We all put our heads under the robes and snuggle deeper into the straw, quickly warming the entire group of travelers.

You can see the community church is not an abandonment of the big church uptown. It was built so the community can worship nearly every Sunday like the Bible commands. That commandment can be broken if you are sick or a particularly bad storm makes even a short trip unsafe. I'm not sure just what number that commandment is, but I think there are ten in all.

I got distracted a bit, but this whole misunderstanding started in Church. This is the one time the ladies can socialize and the men can share their plans for fixing all the trouble caused by the idiots who run our country. We have a preacher, but he didn't go to Bible school – sort of a self-taught saint. He keeps himself alive on his ten dollar salary with a large garden and a milk cow. He punishes us for his poor salary with two hour sermons and lots of shouting and thumping on the pulpit. If he gets wind of any scandals from the after-church socializing, he preaches a whole series of sermons on the topic, sometimes even reading Bible verses about it if he can find any. The series on "Pride Goeth Before A Fall" was prompted by the Knudsons arriving at church in a new Ford automobile. It was owned by a relative visiting from Minneapolis.

We are required to sit still during the whole service, but there is great fun and chasing and teasing among the kids after the benediction. Sunday dinner may not be on the table before suppertime. Sunday is truly a Holy day in this community. We get the preacher for Sunday dinner about once a month. He occasionally shows up at supper time on an ordinary day for a pastoral visit. That man can eat more than two hard-working farm hands. His girth is testimony to years of that activity. He prefers Sunday dinners because mom always roasts a chicken for that special occasion.

Now, back to the issue at hand. Matilda sees me Sunday morning and is shocked to see several bandages on my arms and a big scratch on my cheek. I am still limping a bit after the cow riding incident. She inquires of mom how I got hurt. Mom truthfully tells her she is uncertain of how I was injured. My explanation involved dragons and lions and wolves and bears and had such inconsistency that my own mother doubts she has the whole story. The manure in my hair and all over my torn clothes suggests something happened in the barnyard, but I didn't let out a peep about that. None of my armor bearers doubt a word of my explanations even though they are vague and inconsistent. They all know of my fearless, or rather, courageous forays into the most dangerous situations. My apparent injuries are enough to convince them that I am lucky to be alive.

Matilda's niece is a social worker in superior. Matilda calls her that very day to report a possible case of child abuse. Gertrude calls mom and becomes alarmed when she hears about Knights and a Round Table. She schedules an appointment to interview the family which leaves her even more alarmed. It isn't a simple case of child abuse. Everyone present clearly loves and cares for everyone else in this God-fearing country home.

Uncle Ralph (Merlin) spills the beans when he says that I think I am Sir Lancelot, a Knight of the Round Table. He shows her his magic scepter with the gold knob and cone shaped cardboard hat with the stars and moon on it. He shows her how the dining table can be converted to a Round Table where Sir Lancelot recounts his many deeds of valor. And he shows her the sword with many notches, each representing a significant victory over great beasts. When she asks about my injuries, he admits they are puzzling to him as well since I have been unscathed in all of my other adventures.

Gertrude is certain she knows the truth that is escaping all the family members. Sir Lancelot is crazy! He is so deeply embedded in a delusional system that he engages in self-mutilation to convince others of his bravery. She gets mom really worried since she is a professional social worker and must know what she is talking about. Secretly, mom already wonders if she has a crazy kid on her hands, but she never lets it out. This is the greatest emergency Gertrude had ever seen. According to her, I might commit suicide just to prove I am fighting a dragon. An appointment is made with a psychiatrist. I will be the first person in the whole community who has ever seen a psychiatrist.

We arrive at the doctor's office in Superior the next week, two hours early for our appointment. Uncle Ralph drives mom and me to the doctor because he wants to be sure this whole thing doesn't get out of hand. Mom trusts these professional people far too much. Ralph says "Gertrude is far crazier than Sir Lancelot."

This doctor is a Child Psychiatrist and has degrees and Chamber of Commerce plaques and Lions Club and Moose club plaques all over his wall. He is truly a big Mucky Muck! I am awe stricken by the whole scene. Maybe I will become a Psychiatrist and operate on sick people and tell them how to live forever. This is the sort of inspiration that can change your whole life. Two hours is longer than eternity when there is nothing to do. Mom stares straight ahead with her hands tightly folded in her lap. She is worried. Uncle Ralph watches a fly buzzing between the window and the screen. He finally gets up and opens the window a crack so the fly can escape. Merlin isn't worried at all. He is just bored. I have the great notched sword with me. Gertrude said "Bring the sword. That will be the evidence that convinces the psychiatrist that Sir Lancelot is crazy and a bit dangerous."

I notice a fine toy horse sitting in a corner of the room. I walk around it and examined it closely. I have never seen anything like it. This is the best toy I have ever seen! It has four springs each attached to a supporting frame and to one leg of the horse. It must be very valuable.

The lady at the desk looks up and asks "Would you like to ride on the horse/" I could have hugged her. I just nod my head and grin. I am on the horse immediately swinging my notched sword in mock battle. The horse bounces up and down with my movements. I learn that I can rock it back and forth until the front of the supporting frame lifts from the floor a bit and then slaps back to the floor with a clatter. I can bounce straight up and down causing the entire frame to rise a few inches from the floor and slap back down with an even louder clatter.

Merlin watches me with interest, but mom is a bit alarmed at the noise I am making. She is afraid the doctor will be disturbed. With vigorous effort and lots of coordination I get the toy to hop around the waiting room like it is alive. The door opens and the doctor watches me riding the horse around his waiting room. He motions for me to ride over to him, which I do. Then I sit quietly on my steed awaiting further instruction.

Mom quickly starts to apologize "I'm sorry for all the noise. I'll have him wait in the chair by me." The doctor raises his index finger and waves it back and forth in a clear sign to remain silent. Without saying a word, he beckons me into his office. I dismount and enter with my sword still in hand. He shuts the door and asks "What is that in your hand?"

I answer "This is the sword with which I defeat all enemies of the Johnson Kingdom. I have slain dragons and wolves and bears and defeated a snow monster with this sword. It was made for me by my uncle who is really the magician Merlin. The notches commemorate each of my victories. The significance of the notched sword is that I am able to protect the Kingdom of

Johnson. He nods understanding and says he wants me to take a test.

He comments, "You win a lot don't you."

I answer with one word, "Always!"

He asks, "Aren't you afraid? Monsters and dragons and wild beasts might hurt you."

I answer, "I'm often afraid. If I wasn't afraid, I couldn't be brave. Merlin says 'it is better to be brave than to be fearless.' Besides, Merlin has cast a spell protecting me from harm when I am in danger as I protect others."

The doctor opens a funny book that has no writing or pictures in it. It looks like someone spilled ink in it and slammed the pages shut creating a symmetrical smear of ink with no special representation that I can make out.

He says "What do you see?"

I tell him "It looks like someone spilled ink in your book".

He laughs and then coaches me "Imagine the ink splotch is a poor picture of something. What do you think it might be a picture of?"

I have lots of experience watching clouds change shape until they remind me of a dog or funny face so I am able to comply with his request. Since the blotches are mostly symmetrical, I see more butterflies than anything else.

He asks "Do you see any dragons or demons or scary stuff?"

I answer "Dragons breathe fire and have big bodies and long tails and none of your pictures are even close. Besides, they aren't all that scary when one is protected by Merlin's magic spell. I am more scared of a rotten egg or a cow licking me or sticking my tongue on a cold pump handle or touching the electric fence."

He asks "Do any of the pictures make you think of sex organs?"

I don't understand what he is talking about so he lets that line of thinking go.

When he gets tired of the bad picture game, we go over to a table with lots of colorful blocks of many shapes. I have never seen blocks that aren't square or rectangular so this is very interesting. You can't stack a block on top of a triangle without it tipping over, but you can put two triangles side by side and stack a block on them and keep building a tower. The circles are most useful in a tower lying on their sides and they give the tower interesting features. I decide to build a tower to the ceiling. I can only reach halfway up standing on my chair. The Psychiatrist seems as interested in building towers as I am, but he lets me do all the planning and construction.

After a while, he says "You can keep playing with the blocks while I make a few notes." He goes to his desk where he pulls up a chair on wheels that rocks and swivels and tilts. I have never seen such a chair. I study its features in case I have an opportunity to make something like that for myself. He must be really rich to have such neat blocks and chairs, though his picture book leaves a bit to be desired. He takes out a pad of paper and starts to write a story.

I ask "What are you writing about?

He says, "I am writing a story about you."

I ask, "Can I can take it home for Uncle Ralph to read to me?"

He says, "I'm not a very good writer and it wouldn't be very interesting."

I say, "I agree since you haven' heard any of my best stories".

He stops writing and says "Tell me one of your stories."

I decide to tell him of the day the heifers were retrieved and I got lost in a magic forest while hunting dragons. I assure him that I drove the marauding dragon from the forest and he has not returned to this day. He really gets interested when I tell him how that adventure created an alliance between the Eriksson and Johnson Kingdoms which exists to this very day. He goes back to his writing with a grin on his face and writes faster than ever. He finally finishes and closes the book. We are friends.

We walk back to the waiting room hand in hand.

Mom asks "Do we have to come back?

The psychiatrist says "You can come back anytime to play, but Sir Lancelot doesn't need to see me as a patient again." He then leans forward and whispers something in mom's ear that makes her smile real big and she comes over and hugs me.

Merlin says, "I guess he's not crazy after all."

The psychiatrist laughs and says, "He's crazy all right, but he will be fine if you don't fence him in."

Merlin exclaims, "My words, exactly!"

So, I guess I really am crazy, but no one seems upset about it any more.

FRIER TUCK

The preacher drops by for a pastoral call at about suppertime. We have a fine meal on the table with fish balls and gravy on mashed potatoes. We have canned green beans with bacon pieces for special flavor. Mom opens a jar of canned peaches since the preacher is here. We only canned one bushel of peaches last fall when the co-op got a truckload from Georgia. They cost seventy five cents a bushel and money was tight since the milk check hadn't come yet. The co-op will sell stuff on credit, but King Arthur says he trades high quality goods like butter and rolled oats and eggs or pays cash. He says people get to living beyond their means when they start taking credit. The rest of the peaches were sold by the time we got our milk check.

We use one of the 20 quarts of canned peaches only for company or a special day. We have some carrots cooked in sugar as well. They are called candied carrots and taste as good as candy. We get a fresh loaf of homemade bread with nearly every meal, including this one, and we are allowed to spread as much butter on it as we like as long as we eat the crust too. Strawberry jam and peanut butter are available if you are still hungry after all that. No one spreads the jam and peanut butter on their bread tonight .We can smell the hot apple pie cooling on the counter. When we have company, mom puts extra sugar and cinnamon on the pie crust and puts sugar and cinnamon on the left over crust which is baked beside the pie to be eaten as cookies. She lets us eat them as soon at the pie is taken from the oven. There aren't any left. The preacher arrived too late to get in on that treat.

We all sit at the table and talk for an hour after supper. It is dark out and the preacher says, "It would be better if I spend the night and drove back home in daylight." He goes out to his Model A to get his guitar. We are all waiting for him in the living room on the couch and on pillows thrown on the floor. The big chair is saved for the comfort of our guest. He sings "Suppertime" as a solo to start the singing off. His deep Baritone voice bellows out the lines: "In visions now I hear my mother calling. Come home, come home its supper time. The shadows lengthen fast. Come home, come home its supper time we're going home at last."

The guitar is slightly out of tune and the preacher's singing is a bit flat, but that is overcome by volume. Mom has two songs she loves, and we sing them anytime we have a sing time. One is "The Old Rugged Cross." The other is" 'I'll Fly Away." Merlin gets out his violin and tunes it to the preacher's guitar fixing the flat "E" string on the guitar in the process. We sing both of mom's songs and then do a rousing rendition of "She'll Be Comin' Round the Mountain". King Arthur keeps making up new verses until that song has over forty verses. We catch on and sing along with each new verse. We wind up rolling on the floor and laughing after the verse about the rash she brought and us all doing a scratch, scratch, scratch, scratch.

Merlin turns to me and asks "Do you have any tales to relate at a meeting of the round table?"

I answer "I do!"

Merlin laughs and says "I'm not asking you to marry me just because the preacher is here." Everyone laughs at the joke.

We take the leaves out of the dining room table and pull up an extra chair for the preacher. Merlin goes to get his hat with the stars and moon on it and the Magic scepter. He brings the King's and Queen's crowns and the King's royal bathrobe. I have my great notched sword and hold it high as I announce the reason for this meeting of the Round Table.

The preacher is enthralled over the entire process and asks the dumbest questions like he didn't know anything about the Round Table or Royal Courts or Magicians or anything. By the time we fill him in on the business at hand, I forgot entirely which adventure tale I planned to relate.

The preacher says, "I would like to become a member of the Royal Court instead of just being a guest."

I tell him, "We will be glad to have you join the court, but we will need to discuss the role you will play in court affairs."

Merlin suggests, "You can be court Jester!"

The preacher just frowns at him and says, "That's not funny!"

Guinevere says, "You can be a traveling minstrel"

The preacher rejects that as too effeminate in this fierce world of travail.

I then hit on the perfect part he can play. "He can be Friar Tuck. We need spiritual protection as well as magic to protect us in the dangerous undertakings of Knighthood."

He likes the idea at first, but then says "It won't do. Friar Tuck is Catholic and I am a Born Again, Blood Washed, and Baptized Protestant. I can't go to the dark side!"

We remind him that two of the families in our community church are Catholic, and he is their preacher.

He says, "It is my duty to convert them from their error, and it won't help for me to be pretending to be Catholic. "

Then I tell him, "You can have really neat royal clothes. Friar Tuck will wear a robe with a hood on it and will carry a walking stick and a Bible."

He really likes the part about carrying the Bible since we aren't putting enough emphasis on spreading the gospel as we reminisce about adventures. He asks, "What about Robin Hood?"

I tell him, "We don't have anyone to play Robin Hood, and the Sheriff in these parts isn't evil."

The preacher says, "I will pray about it tonight and give you an answer in the morning."

I don't think he prayed about it too long because I heard him snoring down the hall long before I fell asleep. We're still waiting for his answer.

FIRST LOVE

Sir Lancelot is puzzled by Merlin's comments about carrying mementos into battle. It seems that some knights forget why they are risking their lives as they foray into battle. They need some nice lady to give them a scarf or something to remind them why they should face the danger presented. Sometimes the lady gives the knight a kiss when she sends him off to battle. Everything has its price and putting up with a nice lady kissing you is just one of those things you occasionally have to endure.

I figure those guys must be dumb. Dead people do nothing. Live people do something. Really live people find adventures to make their lives interesting and provide tales to entertain their less adventurous friends and family. I am convinced that the display of courage and experience gained during an adventure is more than enough reason to proceed in even the most threatening situations.

We all have the right to modify our views when new information is discovered. I recieve new information from the most unexpected source one Sunday afternoon. The Iverson's have a visitor for the summer. Violet is five years old and will spend the summer with them while her parents travel to the Philippines for a short term mission trip. Violet is a shy young lady who stays close to her aunt and uncle while the other children chase each other all over the church yard in a spirited game of tag after church. All of the children are wearing their Sunday best clothes which are freshly washed and all the worn out places are neatly patched. Mom says it is respectful to God to wear your best clothes when you are in His presence. Now we also know we have to behave well at all times because God is everywhere we are – makes you a bit embarrassed to take your clothes off to take a bath, but God must be used to that by now.

Violet isn't a pretty girl. She is beautiful! She is exotic having come from Texas, a place of legendary giants like Pecos Bill and Gene Autry. I may become a cowboy if the girls down there are all like Violet. I've only heard her speak a few words, but those words inform me of her melodic voice and fascinating accent. Violet has on exotic clothes. Her dress puffs way out at the bottom, pushed out by dozens of petticoats. She has a white blouse with puffy arms and elastic at the elbows. She stands with all of her weight on one leg like she is posing for a photograph. It would be one fine photo too! I don't know anyone except Aunt Ethel who has a camera, and she only visits a couple of times a year. She brings all of her pictures with her, and we spend a lot of time looking at them when she visits.

I would like this beautiful creature to notice me. I run really fast even when I'm not being chased by whoever is "it". I run dangerously close to the person who is "it" in attempt to spark a chase. I flop down on the grass at the corner of the church where I can study this interesting young lady without being noticed. Uncle Ralph hunkers down next to me and knowingly raises his eyebrows.

He says, "I see you've noticed the new lady in town".

I respond, "I don't like girls much. They're just afraid they'll get dirty if they play in the dirt and they're scared of everything. Do you know how long she will be staying with the Iverson's?"

I am trying to be casual and exhibit disinterest, but I am secretly delighted when he says she is staying all summer. There really is a God who cares for us! I overheard Mom asking my two cousin sisters if they would like Violet to come over to our house for a visit since there are no other children at the Iverson farm.

I say "It is ok with me!" even though I wasn't asked.

I can't believe my good fortune when Mom invites the Iverson's over for supper next Thursday. She recommends they come early "So the kids can play a while before supper." This is the stuff dreams are made of! I pretend like it doesn't make any difference to me.

I ask Mom "How do you spell Violet? Is that the same way the flower and the color are spelled?"

She says "They are all the same but you have to capitalize the "V" if it is a name."

I decide to practice spelling Violet when I get home and I will always capitalize the "V". All the way home I am imagining a walk down the lane towards the woods. I will be a step or two ahead of Violet swinging the great notched sword as I describe the exploits memorialized by each notch on the handle. She will listen with rapt attention and only interrupt occasionally to exclaim how wonderfully brave I must be. She will be dressed in the beautiful gown she wore to church. She will have a Violet scarf around her neck. She will stop us when we are out of sight of everyone else and take off her scarf. My heart is pounding at the thought. She will place the scarf around my neck and kiss me on the cheek as she orders me to wear the scarf on my next great adventure in honor of her.

Mom shakes me awake. I'm in the back seat of the car parked next to the back porch at home. No one else is in the car. Mom says "Come in because dinner is on the table and everyone is waiting for you."

I would really like to slip back into the dream. I was just about to pledge my honor to Violet for the rest of my life, and now I can't return to get that job done. No harm done. I am just rehearsing for next Thursday's visit. That's when my dreams will all come true.

Mom asks "Were you having a nice dream? You were mumbling in your sleep and had a big smile on your face."

I nearly panic for a minute, thinking, "my secret is out." I ask Mom "What was I mumbling about?"

She shrugs her shoulders assuring me that my secret is undiscovered.

I tell her "I needed rest after that exhausting game of tag."

Mom says "I haven't seen you play so hard after church in a long time." She secretly worries because I am usually huddled with a group of boys regaling them with accounts of "imaginary" adventure.

I really have no particular expectation regarding the Iverson's visit next Thursday, but I nearly expose myself when I ask, "How many days it is until Thursday?" for the fifth time by Tuesday afternoon. I realize it isn't tomorrow and it will be during the afternoon of the next day. I can keep track of that without any more questions.

Wednesday after dinner, I get into the sandbox prison with the other kids. I have a plan. I will get into the sandbox with Violet and the others when she comes over tomorrow. I will spend time getting to know her and show her how well I can build sand castles. After she is completely taken with me, I will teach her how to climb out of the sandbox so we can walk down the lane together. My plans get a bit fuzzy after that, but I get a really happy feeling about how wonderful it will be.

You know I'm a man of action, not just a dreamer. I will carry an extra pair of socks in my pocket Thursday. That's the real secret to escaping from the sandbox prison. I will have socks to give Violet so she will not hurt her toes when she climbs out of the sandbox with me. I'm staying in the sandbox with the others today so no one will think I am just getting into the sandbox tomorrow because Violet is there. No one will suspect anything.

Merlin is a wizard, and I think he might be suspicious. I have to be very careful not to tip him off. I borrowed paper and pencil from him on Monday, and he asked me "Are you going to write a letter to Violet?"

That was a close call! I am just going to practice writing "Violet" so I am good at it by Thursday. Can you imagine how bad it would be if I wrote her name in the sand and spelled it wrong?

I really throw him off track by asking "Who's Violet? Oh, now I remember. That's the girl staying with the Iverson's."

Merlin grins like he has some secret way to read minds. I change the topic to what we might have for supper when our guests arrive Thursday.

Every night I drift off to sleep with the picture of Violet and me walking down the lane. Sometimes, she will hold my hand while we walk. I envision her with a soft light behind her making her silhouette shine. Her face fades until I have trouble remembering just what she looks like. I know it is the face of an angel. Maybe all angels look just like her.

Thursday morning lasts longer than most whole weeks. I have the extra pair of socks in my pocket since I first dressed. I put on my Sunday pants, but Mom made me change into my other pants. I pretend I got on the wrong pair by accident. I run ahead of the others to check on eggs in the outside nests. I remind my armor bearers of each adventure memorialized by a notch on the great notched sword. I am rehearsing for this afternoon and don't want to forget any details. After dinner, we all get into the sandbox prison so Mom doesn't have to watch us while she gets ready for company. I made no attempt to climb out of the prison yesterday so she thought I might stay in again. She mentioned that my socks wouldn't get full of sand if I left them in my shoes like the others, but I said my feet get cold and left them on.

The Iverson's pickup comes up the driveway and parks next to our car. Violet is seated in the middle. She is wearing bib overalls and a red T shirt. She doesn't have a scarf to put around my neck. I can adapt to all that. I have to adjust my imaginary picture to allow for more ordinary clothes. She looks a lot more like my two girl cousins dressed that way, but I know there is something really different about this young lady.

Mom walks over to the sand box prison and introduces each of my armor bearers to Violet and introduces me as Sir Lancelot. The Iversons laugh at that and Violet smiles a beautiful smile. I'm really pleased with that introduction and invite Violet into our castle. It wouldn't be good to point out the fact that it is really a prison. The gate is locked and Mom and Mrs. Iverson go into the house while Mr. Iverson walks over to join Merlin and King Arthur where they are fixing a broken board on the pasture gate.

I am preparing for the greatest adventure of my life. Violet is given her pick of the tools for sand excavation, and I begin work on a great sand castle. After the walls are made, I scoop sand from around them to form a moat. The damp sand thus obtained can be packed into an old metal tumbler to make towers at the corners of the castle. Violet tries to build one of the towers higher and the whole tower collapses. I hide my exasperation. She is only a girl and girls aren't usually good builders.

It is really hard to repair the collapsing castle, so it is leveled by the whole crew. I smooth out a big place on the pile of sand castle ruins. I take a tarnished old butter knife and carefully spell out "Violet" while everyone watches. I'm really good at it because I've practiced a lot. Only three of us know what I've done. My older brother can read, and Violet recognizes her name. When the others ask what it says, Violet says, "That's my name!" I can tell she is pleased because she clasps her hands together and looks at me with an admiring smile.

Violet traces the letters with her finger as she says each letter aloud. Her finger messes up my carefully executed artwork, but I let that go since Violet is doing the damage unintentionally. I would have clobbered any of the others if they had messed up my castle and pretty writing. Violet asks what my name is and I respond "Sir Lancelot."

She laughs and says, "No, what's your real name?" I glare at my armor bearers and no one decides to ruin my day in fear that I might ruin theirs. Since that isn't going anywhere, Violet asks me how to spell Sir Lancelot.

I have to confess," I don't know."

I never thought of names as something to write down before I met Violet. She wants to write my name and I let her down. She smoothes the sand out, erasing her name and writes "serlandalot." I'm pretty sure that is wrong, but I don't know how to fix it.

I mention "Names have to start with a capital letter."

Violet seems miffed at the correction and wipes the whole name off the sand pile. Everyone begins their own sand project with roads and tunnels and ditches appearing and disappearing with little overall cooperation. I watch Violet to see if she starts a project to which I can contribute. She draws a big circle and puts two smaller circles inside. When she makes a semicircle mouth, I can tell it is a face she is making. I watch as she makes a tiny stick figure under the face.

I ask "Who are you trying to draw?"

She says "It's a drawing of you."

I think it is a complement until she says "You have a big head."

I tell her "It can't be me because Sir Lancelot always carries a great notched sword with which to fight dragons and lions and wolves and stuff."

She responds with a single word, "Poo!"

I decide not to start any of the adventure stories I was about to tell her. She may not appreciate bravery. My elaborate plans for the day are in real trouble. I pull out my ace in the hole. I tell Violet, "You aren't really in a castle. You are in the sand box prison."

She looks around and everyone nods their head in agreement. She is so downcast that I feel guilty for the revelation. I immediately state "I have an escape plan."

She looks at me with renewed interest and everyone stops their projects to see what is going to happen. They haven't seen me escape from the sand box in many weeks since the adults decided not to lock me in there any more.

I explain "One can scale the wire at the corner if they have socks on to keep their feet from being hurt by the wire." I get the extra socks out of my pocket to the amazement of everyone present. I still have my own socks on.

As I help Violet put the socks on her bare feet, all of my earlier disappointment vanishes. I'm back in charge of my fate and the day will proceed as planned. I show

Violet how to put her toes in the wire and climb out of the enclosure. I then scramble up the wire and swing over the post and scramble down the outside like a monkey in a zoo.

Violet puts her foot into the wire and grabs the wire above her. The wire hurts her fingers as she pulls herself up the first step and she lets go falling back into the sand box. I can't get her to try again. She says she likes it in the sand box because all the toys and playmates are there.

What about me? I have romance and adventure in mind, and Violet would rather stay in the sand box prison.

Disappointment is a word which cannot encompass my feelings. I might quit the whole adventure business. I'm surely not going to save any maidens in distress. They're not worth saving. At least I won't have to put up with wearing a sissy scarf and putting up with a kiss if I do go off on another adventure. I head over to the ditch where a little water stands most of the time on the other side of the driveway. I get pretty dirty chasing a small green frog, but I finally capture him. He is pretty interesting so I bring him to the sand box prison to show the others.

Violet sees me coming. She points at me and laughs. The armor bearers laugh with her because I have mud on my face. I change my mind about showing them the interesting frog. I put him through the chicken wire dropping him in the sand box and warn everyone that he is poisonous. All three girls start to scream, and the boys move away from the menacing creature.

That will teach them to laugh at Sir Lancelot. The frog isn't interested in scaring a bunch of kids. He hops out of the enclosure and escapes in the direction of his marshy home.

Mom and Mrs. Iverson run out of the kitchen to see what has caused the commotion. I'm a muddy mess. The armor bearers tell mom that I put a poison frog in the sand box. Mrs. Iverson asks Violet what she has on her feet and my escape scheme is uncovered. Mom makes me come in to clean up, and I'm not allowed to go out until supper is over.

I'm through with girls! That's a lesson that seems to be learned too late for most of us guys. Merlin says this was my most dangerous adventure, and it deserves a notch on my sword. He reads me a story about an old time hero who had the same experience on an island full of sirens.

PARATROOOPER SCHOOL

Sir Lancelot is thinking it would be useful to learn how to fly. Dragons fly. Birds fly. Even bugs fly. Flying can't be that hard. If you run real fast and jump as you get near a ditch, you can fly over the ditch. It seems that flying is simply a matter of extending what comes naturally. Soldiers jump out of airplanes and fly a long way with the help of a parachute. These guys are big and heavy and carry a lot of gear. It should be a lot easier for a thirty-eight pound five year old to fly.

I have had several experiences of falling which are a bit unpleasant. They are worse if you land in the wrong places. It seems that planning a safe landing should be the first consideration before beginning a flight. I love to jump on the bed, because the landing place is soft. You can climb up on the dresser and fly longer before landing, and it is even more fun. I broke the boards that hold the bed springs, and Mom says I can't jump on the bed any more.

I'm ok with that restriction because I have flying plans that go far beyond those first fun experiments. I ask Merlin how parachutes work and he shows me the nitty-gritty of parachute design. He ties the four corners of a silk scarf to long strings which he ties to a heavy steel nut from the hardware drawer. We go out on the porch and he wraps the stuff real tight in his hand. He throws the ball of cloth and steel nut high in the air and the scarf spreads out and the nut drifts lazily to the ground.

I ponder the physics of flight a lot. It seems that you can fly longer if you start higher. It seems that the parachute canopy must be bigger and lighter than the load. I imagine myself being shot from a big cannon instead of being thrown into the air like Merlin did with his model parachute. I saw a billboard advertizing a circus with a man being shot from a cannon. I don't think there are any of those around the Kingdom of Johnson. I pick a white puffy ripe dandelion and blow the seeds off. They don't fall at all. They just drift on across the yard in the breeze. I don't just want to have my fall slowed by a parachute. I want to drift on the breeze like a dandelion seed.

I ask Merlin "Is an umbrella like a parachute?"

He rubs his chin before answering and says, "There are a lot of similarities." Then he laughs and says, "The World War II paratroopers should have had large umbrellas instead of parachutes so the Germans would know the English were coming."

I don't see why that would identify them as English, but it seems pretty funny to Merlin. I have only seen one umbrella up close. I have seen pictures of people carrying them. In fact there is a play called Mary Poppins where a lady is drifting on the breeze hanging onto an umbrella. The plans are falling in place.

I will start my flying research with an umbrella. We have a black umbrella stored behind the storm door on the back porch. I have never seen it in use even when it is raining, but we keep it in case it is needed. I think I can take the umbrella out to the hay mow of the barn with no one noticing. There is a large door at the top of the haymow where hay is loaded in from wagons by a big fork. The hay travels into the barn and is dropped when the trip rope is pulled. The hay forks and trip rope and pulleys are attached to a rail that runs across the roof of the haymow. The Hay pile in the barn is nearly up to the door where the hay is brought in. It is easy to get on the ledge by this door and look out. It is a long way down to the lane below.

Mom has a picture of Mary Poppins holding the umbrella in her right hand as she floats above the countryside. I study this picture to be sure I understand the technique. I could cover a lot of ground searching for dragons if I was drifting along under an umbrella like a giant dandelion seed. I have no flying experience so I decide that I should make special landing preparations for the first few flights.

I recruit the entire squad of armor bearers to prepare the landing site. We throw hay out of the barn and pile it below the door to the haymow. We run and jump in the air landing on the hay pile. This is great fun, but bigger things are in store. When the hay pile is really high I tell everyone that I am going to make my first flight out of the haymow. They have to stop jumping on the hay pile because they keep knocking it down and I may need a lot of cushion for my landing.

Then I reveal the great secret. I take the umbrella from the corner where I placed it a couple of days ago and open it up. I have never seen the umbrella opened before. It is gigantic. Lying on its side, the edge is twice as tall as I am. The handle is longer than I am tall. This should be a great parachute. I begin to worry that I will drift out across the pasture and into the woods where I will get tangled in the top of a big tree. If it doesn't let me float to the ground I may not be able to get down. Fearlessness is not bravery! I am fearful, but I am also brave. Even if I do wind up a long way from home, I can get someone to come and get me and I will be a hero. We might get my aunt with the camera to come over and take a picture of me flying around the Kingdom.

As I step onto the ledge above the hay pile, I can feel the slight breeze trying to pull the umbrella from my grip. This is a powerful flying machine. I shout "Stand clear!" as I leap from the barn so the umbrella will not catch on the ledge. I'm not quite sure what happened next because the umbrella nearly jerks my arm from its socket and I am barely able to hold on with both hands. The umbrella turns inside out just before I hit the hay pile. We hadn't piled the hay nearly high enough. My knees hit my chin and I roll forward onto the broken umbrella. I can't breathe or answer anyone for several seconds after my landing.

The armor bearers show their true loyalty today. They spend the rest of the morning helping me carry the hay back in the barn. We spend a lot of time trying to bend the broken umbrella ribs straight and fold it up like we found it. When the cloth is wrapped around the broken ribs and folded as good as we can get it, the umbrella hardly looks any different than it did before my flight. I put the umbrella back behind the door where I found it.

I am nearly found out the next Sunday when we are about to get in the car for church. Merlin asks mom if she would like the umbrella since it is raining. She says not to bother. There is no reason to act uppity just because it is sprinkling a little. I'm not ready to explain the umbrella damage just now.

BIOLOGY 101

Sir Lancelot can probably teach a high school biology course. The Kingdom of Johnson is a close partnership between nature and man. The rhythms of the seasons determine the appropriate activity for the inhabitants. Each season is spent preparing for the next. Spring demands preparation of the soil, planting, and fertilizing. Weed and pest control are the early focus in summer followed by harvest of each crop in its time and replanting of some crops. Fall is notable for harvest and preparation for winter. Cutting wood for heating and canning and storing of food and crops is a time of celebration. Winter is the time crop rotation and land use planning determines the activity to occur when spring arrives. The shorter days in winter encourage socializing around the fire during the long evenings.

Sir Lancelot, out of necessity, is very observant. I have observed five full cycles and need no instruction to advise me about the need of preparation for the future. Merlin says he is interested in the future because that is where he plans to spend the rest of his life. Sir Lancelot figures Camelot is nothing like the Kingdom of Johnson. It must be summer always in Camelot and no one has to prepare for winter. That's why they spend all of their time with feasts and pageants and crusades and stuff.

Sir Lancelot is a lot bigger than last year and hopes to be included in more of the fun preparations for winter. King Arthur and Merlin take a wagon to the woods where they cut logs to sell to the saw mill in Solen Springs. The lumber company sends a truck and loader to load the log pile for its trip to the saw mill. They bring loads of slab wood back from the saw mill to be cut up for firewood. The wood pile is a great place to play beside the machine shed. When harvest is done, Merlin and King Arthur cut the slab wood into short lengths that fit into the fireplace and furnace. If the slabs are too wide, they are chopped in half so they are easier to carry and put in the fire.

The smaller wood pieces stack better in the wood box as well. Last fall and winter I helped fill the wood box, but I could only carry one piece of wood at a time. Merlin and King Arthur each carry a whole armload of wood each trip to the wood box. When the wood box is full, they let me put the last piece in. Then they report to Guinevere that Sir Lancelot is done filling the wood box. I really like to work hard when I get credit for my work and even for work done by others.

A huge saw is hooked to the tractor by a long flat belt and two big people are needed to push the slab wood through the saw. I have to stay in the yard to watch the wood being cut so I won't get hurt. I am telling you about the wood cutting so you will understand why I like to play by the pile of slab wood. The wood has been cut in this same place for hundreds or maybe even thousands of years. The sawdust from cutting the wood is a really deep pile that just gets kicked away when it gets so high it is in the way.

Sawdust is interesting stuff. It is soft when you jump into a pile of it. We sometimes build a big pile of sawdust near the slab wood and climb really high and jump into the sawdust while shouting "Geronimo!" I don't know why we shout that, but that's what you are supposed to do when you jump off something. I shouted "Geronimo!" when I jumped out of the hay mow with the umbrella. Mom says "Traditions are what keep us doing the right thing." You want to be doing the right thing when you jump off something high.

I was going to tell you about biology and got sidetracked. Now you might think I'm going to talk about the birds and the bees, but that's pretty simple stuff. We live on a farm. We know chickens won't lay eggs unless there is a rooster making them do their job and bees make honey to feed the eggs and bugs that turn into bees. We know the cows won't give milk unless the bulls make them have a calf once in a while so they make milk for the calf even when he doesn't need any more. Merlin says all the animals we keep to help feed and clothe us are domestic animals. It's pretty easy to figure out what they do because we are always keeping and eye on them. We protect them from bad weather and other danger and feed them if they are hungry.

The wild animals are the interesting ones to find out about. They figure out ways to take care of themselves, and they don't hang around so you can watch them do it. I caught a big bullfrog in the swampy ditch across the driveway. He makes really funny sounds, and his throat swells up and vibrates when he makes that noise. I named him "Jeff." Merlin agreed to help me make a cage for Jeff so I can learn about frog biology.

We pound four sticks in the ground and wrap screen around the sticks high enough so Jeff can't jump out. We dig a pond and put a piece of oilcloth in the bottom so it holds water. I carry a lot of water in an empty paint can to fill the pond. I put a lot of grass and two rocks in the frog pen so Jeff feels at home.

Merlin says, "Jeff has the finest frog house in the county." I want to feed Jeff, but I don't know what frogs eat. Merlin says, "He eats bugs and flies."

I tell Merlin, "I will get a fly swatter and collect supper for Jeff."

Merlin replies, "Frogs won't eat dead bugs. We have to get some flies to come to Jeff's frog house."

I ask Merlin, "Now what do you think I could tell a fly that would get him to come to Jeff's frog house so Jeff can eat him? I don't even know how to talk fly talk. You are a wizard. Maybe you can put a spell on some flies to get them to come over."

Merlin says, "I can do just that." He goes to the barn and gets a scoop of fresh manure that has flies swarming around it and dumps it in a corner of Jeff's frog house. I don't think Jeff will be a bit more pleased about the smell in his new home than I am.

Merlin really is a wizard. Some of the flies he talked to come over to check out Jeff's frog house. I think they like the smell of the manure because they hang around that stuff a lot. Jeff hops over near the manure pile in his house and scares the flies away. Jeff sits real still and the flies come back to check things out. What happens next is so amazing I have to see it several times before I figure out what happens. The flies are sitting on the manure pile and then one jumps into Jeff's mouth. Jeff swallows the crazy fly and another one jumps into his mouth. They must like being eaten by a frog. I

82

wonder how Jeff gets to eat when Merlin doesn't talk the flies into being a frog meal.

Jeff hops into his pond when he is full and just sits there keeping cool. I get bored watching him do nothing, so I head over to the sawdust pile to catch a snake. I think Jeff would like company. This might surprise you, but garter snakes and copper bellies like to make holes in the sawdust pile. They live in these holes and come out to lie in the sun sometimes. They either dive into a hole or scoot off into the grass when you get near them. They don't have any feet, but they can move really fast when they are trying to hide from you. I can't see what makes them move, but it entails a lot of squirming and doesn't make any noise. Snakes don't talk at all. Mom says they hiss, but I have never seen one hiss.

Mom is afraid of snakes. That is really funny because they are afraid of people. We catch them when we pile sawdust up to jump in. If they are in their hole when we scoop up a pile of sawdust, they aren't sure what to do so they let us hold them and they don't even try to get away when we let them rest on our arms. The big snakes are about as long as your arm, but they are too fast to catch. The little ones don't move as fast and don't seem to mind being held. They still don't stay around if you put them down. Mom says we can't bring snakes in the house. Otherwise, I might try to tame one for a pet and let him take a nap with me. I have studied a snake on my arm as he moves and it is like magic. Merlin says most of nature is like magic.

I figure Jeff will like a garter snake named George, so I put George in the frog house with Jeff. Jeff just sits in his pond and doesn't even look at George. I want them to be friends so I reach for Jeff to put him next to George, but he hops away from me like he is too snooty to be friends with anybody. George doesn't seem to be interested in making friends either. He glides along the edge of the screen and finds a place where he can duck his head under the screen and wriggles right out of the frog house. I pick him up just as he is out of the frog house and put him back. I can see he isn't going to make friends with Jeff and I won't be able to keep him in the frog house unless I guard it the whole time. I understand George very well. I have the same feeling in the sandbox prison. I like it in the sandbox well enough, but I'd rather be out. This time I let George scurry toward the ditch across the driveway after he crawls under the screen again.

That makes me wonder if Jeff is happy in his frog house. I decide to check it out by lifting the screen at one corner high enough so Jeff can crawl out if he wants to. Jeff seems contented to stay in his frog house. I have to go in for supper and will come back to play with Jeff tomorrow.

I come over to the frog house first thing before even looking for the outside eggs. All of my armor bearers come with me because they didn't meet Jeff yesterday. I tell them about the enchanted flies and how snakes don't like to play with frogs. They are anxious to meet Jeff, but Jeff is gone.

I learned a lot about nature and I'll teach it to you in case no one has observed this before. Flies like being eaten by frogs. Snakes and frogs don't want to be friends. Domestic animals like to stay in their pens like the armor bearers and girls like to stay in the sandbox prison. Snakes don't walk, they get around like magic. You don't have to be afraid of snakes because they are afraid of you. Wild animals are a lot like me. They prefer to get out of their pens and do whatever they feel like doing instead of what you want them to do. Merlin says I will be a biologist when I grow up, but I don't know what that is.

LOST AGAIN

Everyone in the Kingdom except Merlin is going to Superior for a day of resupply and recreation. King Arthur has a secret plan to replace our worn out Model A with new car. "New car" means a car which is a few years newer and "new" to us. We pack a lunch so we can have a picnic at the roadside picnic table next to the lake at Solen Springs on the way home.

Mom can really put a feast together for a picnic. She packs a red checkered oil cloth table cover and old sheets to cover the bench seats. We make such a nice picture when we have a picnic that it would be a fine magazine cover. Mom has style. She packs sugar and two packages of red Kool-Aid just because it makes the table pretty to look at. She packs a glass pitcher and tumblers wrapped in socks so they won't break. We have aluminum tumblers, but they don't suit Mom's sense of style.

A real blow-out is planned for the day. Mom has packed a quart of canned peaches, the last one to survive since last fall's canning. She sliced the center section from a ham hanging in the smokehouse. We are going to buy a loaf of bread in town and have rare "bought bread" ham sandwiches at the picnic. A crock full of baked beans with bits of fat back flavoring baked in the oven all day yesterday. The smell of the beans mixed with the usual homemade bread aroma kept us all aware of tomorrow's adventure and feast. A large bowl of potato salad and a jar of pickles ensures that enough food is present to feed added guests if thy happen by during our picnic.

King Arthur and Merlin spend a while in secret conference after chores are done. We pack two boxes of picnic supplies on the floor in the back seat of the Model A. The boxes are covered with clean dish towels. A milk pail with two bars of lye soap and several towels is placed next to the boxes. Mom will not allow dirty passengers or dishes back into the car after the picnic. We can play at Solen Springs and have plenty of time for clean up afterwards. We don't have to be back in time for evening chores since Merlin is going to milk by himself tonight.

The car is packed. King Arthur and Guinevere are settled in the front seat with the two smallest armor bearers between them. The other five including me are crowded into the back seat with stern warnings not to get our feet onto the boxes of picnic supplies. You can stand on the back seat with your hands on the back of the front seat to see out the front window and be first to notice interesting sights on the trip.

This is actually the safest position as everyone is braced in case the car lurches in a rut in the road or a quick braking is needed to avoid domestic animals in the road. Neighbors consider it a personal attack if you run over one of their chickens even if it is an accident. Walter Nolen was driving by our house drunk and hit a pig sunning in the road. We had to tow his car into our yard with the tractor. Dad made him help butcher the pig before giving him a ride home. He had to sign a paper agreeing not to drive drunk before Dad let him have his car back even after Al Gentry had the radiator and front end fixed. Law enforcement is best left under local control.

The most interesting part of the trip to town begins when we turn onto Highway 2 which has a dashed centerline painted on the paved surface. There are businesses like gas stations and feed stores and blacksmith shops along the highway. The thing that makes this part of the trip interesting is the signs. Rich people build big signs and print lots of things on them and paint big pictures of products they think are good for you to buy. We use the signs to play the alphabet game. Mom reminds us of the next letter in the alphabet and we all try to be first to see that letter on the next sign. Sometimes we get three or four sequential letters on one sign. We all point out the turnoff to Solen Springs as we pass County P.

Our first stop is at the Hardware store where Dad hands a list to Don Jackson who rummages around in the big shed behind the store counter. He comes back with a roll of barbed wire and some gate hasps and a can of WD-40. He goes back to get the box of nails and a new axe handle while the other stuff is loaded onto the floor of the back seat completely filling the space in front of the seat. The box of nails will have to sit beside Mom's purse on the floor in front.

We then drive over to the used car lot next to the Chevrolet garage. Mom asks if we shouldn't go to the Ford garage if the car needs something. Dad says he and Uncle Ralph have been thinking about a new bigger car that has a trunk and he just wants to see what is available. This is a really neat place. Red, white and blue pennants with the Chevrolet bow tie emblem are flown from a dozen poles along the street in front of the used cars. A big sign says the cars are on special sale for big discounts and trade-ins are needed for their inventory. This must be a really good time to trade cars.

All seven kids wander around the cars. We look over, under, and around the cars. We name the ones we recognize. There is a section of three Model A cars that look just like our car, except the paint is shinier, and they have colorful signs in the front window. An old Studebaker commander has a box on the back that could carry lots of stuff, but it has a cloth roof and Dad says he is looking for a turret top. He says it has to have good tires, a big trunk, and lots of space inside.

The salesman says he has the perfect car and shows Dad a 1939 Buick Special. It has a powerful straight eight flat head engine which is second only to the 12 cylinder engines in the top of the line Packards and Cadillacs. Those cars cost over two thousand dollars and aren't being considered. The Buick's heater will keep the windshield clear and the car warm in the coldest weather. Dad and the salesman get in the Buick for a test drive, and we watch the great shiny beast disappear around the corner.

We are all hoping we can ride home in that automobile this afternoon. Mom sits on the steps to the Sales office to wait and watch us. I have been allowed to bring the great notched sword with the proviso that it remain safely tucked in my belt. I could have organized a charge on the enemy hiding behind the sales office, but one cannot effectively enter battle with his sword in its scabbard. We all wander around the cars looking for something to do.

I notice a rock in the gravel-covered car lot bigger and rounder than most. I begin to kick it ahead of me as I snake in and out between the cars. I kick the rock onto the sidewalk where it rolls better. Mom walks past me and I follow along behind her, keeping my eye on my rock I named "Joe." It is sort of hard keeping up because Mom is walking faster than usual. I have to zig and zag to keep Joe on track. Mom stops at a corner street crossing and I look up to see what she might be planning.

To my horror I find myself looking up at a complete stranger. Her coat is the same color as Mom's. She is puzzled to find a strange kid kicking a rock down the sidewalk behind her. I don't know where we are. We turned several corners while I was following her. I look around and see nothing familiar. I am lost! I start to cry.

The nice lady asks, "What is wrong?"

I blurt out,"I am lost!"

She asks, "Where do you live?"

I tell her, "I live in the Kingdom of Johnson."

She laughs and asks, "What is your name?"

I reply, "I'm Sir Lancelot." I get out my sword to emphasize the point. I bend over and pick up my rock and say, "his name is 'Joe'." I put Joe in my pocket.

The nice lady says, "I bet Joe doesn't know the way home either." She doesn't seem frightened at all.

I ask, "Can you help me find my parents?"

The nice lady takes me by the hand after I put the great notched sword back in my belt. She says, "I can help you find your parents. I have friends who know where everyone belongs." She then walks a couple of blocks and enters a drug store where she has a long conversation with a man who laughs a lot.

I ask, "Do you know where my parents are?"

He says, "I can find out." He then goes to an icebox behind the counter and makes an ice-cream cone for me. He tells the nice lady, "I will get him back to his parents." She leaves the store.

I sit on the stool at the counter eating my ice-cream cone thinking that being lost isn't the worst thing that can happen to a brave knight. This might turn into one of my more exciting adventures. The last time I was lost in the magic forest I had no one to help me until I met the Eriksons. That was a lot more frightening.

The man behind the counter picks up a telephone and talks to someone. We have a telephone, so I assume he must be telling my parents where I am. He hangs up the phone and comes around the counter to sit on the stool next to me.

He asks, "Do you like the ice cream?"

I answer, "I surely do!"

He says, "I called some friends to take you back to your parents."

I think he is the best conversationalist I have ever met. He talks with me for a long time and is so skillful at evading questions that I haven't learned a thing about how I'm to get home.

A policeman comes in the door. This guy is huge. He has on a blue uniform with a shiny badge on his shirt. He has a real gun on his belt. His hat has a shiny bill on it unlike any other hat I've ever seen. He has another badge on his hat. He seems really happy about something. The drugstore man sure does laugh a lot. He gets the policeman laughing too. I don't know what is so funny, but the atmosphere is infectious and I start to laugh as well.

They turn to me, and the policeman says, "I came to get you home." The drugstore man sure must be important to have a friend who is a policeman.

I ask the policeman, "Do you know where I live?"

He says, "I understand that you are one of the knights from the Kingdom of Johnson." Then he and the drugstore man start laughing again.

I quickly correct him. I inform him, "I am Sir Lancelot, the ONLY knight in the Kingdom of Johnson. I inform him, "It is my solemn duty to protect the kingdom from dragons and wild beasts." I pull out the great notched sword and explain, "Each notch represents victory over a dangerous foe including dragons, lions, wolves and an ice monster." I tell him, "I have six armor bearers and King Arthur, Guinevere and Merlin residing in the kingdom with me."

The drug store man puts his head in his arms and starts to shake as he laughs. I would wonder if this is a crazy man except he has a friend who is a policeman.

The policeman asks, "Do you like ice cream?" I nod my head vigorously. These are some of the nicest people I have ever met. He tells the drugstore man to make me an ice cream cone and gives him a nickel. The drugstore man refuses the money and makes me another ice cream cone.

I tell him "Thank you. Are you always this happy?"

He says, "My nickname is 'Happy.'"

I tell him "I know another guy with that name, but he is a dwarf." I have to laugh along with them again because they seem delighted to know there is another "Happy" even if he is a dwarf.

The policeman takes me by the hand and says I can go for a ride in his police car. He waves goodbye to Happy and we get into the police car. It has a red light on the roof. I ask, "How does it work?" The policeman lets me get out watch the light flash after he turns it on. I ask, "Does this car have a siren?" I am greeted by a loud high-pitched wail.

The drugstore man comes out to wave goodbye to us again as we climb back into the police car to leave. The policeman has a two way radio in his car and calls the police station to say he is on his way downtown with an errant knight. He hands me the mike and shows me how to press the transmit button. He tells me, "Give them your name and address."

I press the button and announce, "Sir Lancelot from the Kingdom of Johnson is on the way downtown to meet King Arthur and Guinevere and my armor bearers."

The policeman says, "Let go of the transmit button so you can listen to the other policemen at the station." They aren't saying anything. Policemen laugh a lot.

They ask, "George, is he armed?" (That must be my policeman's name, because he picks up the mike and answers.) He says, "He has a sword, but don't worry because we are on the same side."

George and I walk into the police station hand-in-hand. A whole bunch of policemen and a couple of pretty ladies are standing in front of a long counter. They shout, "Welcome Sir Lancelot!" and clap their hands. I pull out the great notched sword and wave it in the air in greeting. The whole crowd roars in laughter. George and I join right in. Policemen sure have a lot of fun. I am pleased to see how my fame has spread beyond the Kingdom. Merlin will want to carve another notch on my sword to commemorate this day even though no conquest is involved.

I take the seat offered at a heavy oak table surrounded by heavy oak chairs. A nice lady with a badge on her shirt asks me a lot of questions, but I don't know the answer to most of them. She writes a lot of stuff on her tablet anyway. She says she is a policewoman. I never heard of a policewoman before, but she says there are lots of them.

I ask, "Where is your gun?"

She says, "I leave it in my desk when I talk to knights so there won't be any needless battles."

I tell her, "I keep my sword with me most all the time because it's too late if you need it and don't have it with you."

She says, "You would make a good policeman."

I will consider that when I grow up. Policemen seem to have a lot of fun, and the policewomen are really nice ladies.

I ask, "Where do you keep the electric chair?"

She points to a big chair next to a desk with a sign on it. The sign reads "Captain Willis." I can't read the sign, but the policewoman reads it to me.

I ask, "Is Captain Willis the one who pushes the button to electrocute criminals?" She says, "Captain Willis will push the button any time he feels like it!"

I think it would be fun to be the one to push the button on the electric chair. If I am offered a seat in one of those big chairs in a police station, I will turn it down in case Captain Willis is in a bad mood.

George comes over to say King Arthur and his court are on the way to retrieve Sir Lancelot. I am waiting at the door as they walk in and Mom hugs me so hard I can't breathe. Dad is trying to thank the policemen for finding me, but they keep laughing a lot and Dad laughs along with them. If you ever get a chance to go to a police station, you will find it is a lot more fun than you would expect.

I get into the Model A, disappointed that it isn't a Buick. I want to find out what happened at the car lot in my absence, but everyone else wants to find out what happened to me. The conversation is so disjointed that it is hard to put it all together. I show them "Joe" and say we should take him back to his home at the car lot.

Dad agrees, and that's just what we do. Two of the armor bearers say they are going to get lost at their first opportunity when they hear about all the nice people I met and the two ice-cream cones.

The salesman comes running to the car as we pull in to drop Joe off at his home. You would think we were the salesman's best friends who haven't visited in a long time. I realize he is only interested in my welfare. He asks if the missing kid has been found. He wants to know if I was kidnapped. He says the Ford dealer isn't above dirty tricks to keep him from selling a car.

It seems Dad liked the Buick well enough, but all discussion of automobile purchases stopped when my absence was discovered. Everyone walked around several blocks asking if anyone had seen me. Even the salesman had been looking for me, though he wouldn't know me if he saw me.

When the police were notified of my absence, they said, "We found a lost kid, but the name is wrong. They found a "Sir Lancelot of the Kingdom of Johnson." Mom cried, but Dad laughed. The salesman wants to talk about the Buick deal, but Dad says he has more important business in mind. Now that we're back the salesman is assuming we are here to buy the Buick. I thought he would be glad to hear we brought the rock back and I was safe, but that doesn't seem to interest him any more.

Dad gets back into the Model A to start home, and it looks like the salesman is going to cry. He sure can change his mood easily. I remember him jumping up and down and welcoming us back just a few minutes ago. He puts his foot on the running board of the Model A and leans in to quietly present his "Last" and "Best" offer. He tells Dad, "I will allow another $25 trade in on the Model A. I have a lot of demand for Model As from other customers." That brings the offered trade in to $125 for the Model A. Dad had been known to offer the car to several previous interested neighbors for $75. The Buick is a bit pricey at $600, but it is really shiny and has a huge trunk and powerful engine. Dad says, "I am willing to reconsider the Buick, but I must be able to take the family for a ride to get their opinion." The salesman is reluctant but hurriedly agrees when Dad starts the engine on the Model A.

We all cheer and climb into the Buick. Dad loads all the stuff from the hardware store and picnic supplies into the Buick's huge trunk. The five back seat kids are instructed to sit on the seat. The four front seat passengers have lots of room sitting side-by-side.

Mom asks, "Why did we load all our stuff in the Buick when we don't even know if we will buy it?"

Dad points out, "We all have room to be seated comfortably and nothing is stored on the floor in front of the seats." He heads out onto highway 2 and accelerates to 60 mph. The Model A starts to shake at 50 mph and won't get over 55 mph unless it is going downhill.

Dad turns the heater on full blast and the car gets hot inside even though it is summer. He says, "That would really feel good in the winter time."

Mom talks about milk prices and the cost of sugar and flour and rising taxes and lots of other irrelevant stuff. Dad suggests the big trunk would save driving the truck to town at times, and this large powerful car could even pull a trailer for hauling stuff about. They never talk a bit about buying the car or not, but some secret agreement must have been reached. When we get back to the car lot, Dad goes in to write a check and do some paperwork. The salesman comes out to change the license plate from the Model A to the Buick.

We arrive back at the kingdom of Johnson after dark. Merlin is done with chores and comes out to see the new car. We all talk at once. Mom is talking about the wonderful picnic at Solen Springs Lake while Dad extols the features of the Buick. Meanwhile, I describe the happy policemen and the electric chair and two ice-cream cones from "Happy" – not the Dwarf. Merlin knows he has really missed some adventure, but it's bed time and we will get the details another day.

He asks me, "Why did you go to the police station?" No one mentioned that I was lost. Getting lost isn't a particularly brave thing to do so I'm not sure how I'm going to work around that detail when I fill in the story of the trip to Superior.

"Good night, Merlin. I think I may become a policeman when I grow up. I needed to see what policemen do in case I want to be one."

SKUNKED

Just in case some grownups read this stuff, I will define some terms they may not understand correctly. "Dibs" means "I saw it first so I get the reward of discovery even if another is quicker at grabbing it." If I see a penny lying on the ground that no one just dropped, I will say "dibs" and point at it so everyone can share the enjoyment of my discovery. Commonly, someone closer to the treasure will grab it and hold it up for all to see since there is satisfaction in being first to touch treasure. The rule is clear, however, that no matter who picks the treasure up, it is mine unless we discover the true owner to whom it must then be returned.

"Last one in is a rotten egg" is not called in order to label anyone. It just means that we have to go in anyway so we might as well race in and get a little fun out of the deal. You should never call "last one in is a rotten egg" unless there is someone slower than you in the group. It is undignified to issue a challenge and then lose. A "double dare" is exactly the same as a "dare" and a "double dog dare." They all get you the same credit for bravery or foolhardiness as the case may be if you take the challenge. I think adults who once knew the meanings of these things lose the nuances when they grow up and quit learning things.

"NO" can mean a lot of things depending on the tone and volume of the word. I like to think it means you can go ahead and do it if you want, but there will be consequences. I get sidetracked sometimes because the

99

undisciplined mind tends to lose focus. Merlin says I have an undisciplined mind, but that's a good thing or I would be dangerous. Makes no sense to me, but he's a wizard and doesn't make sense a lot of the time. Mom tells me that, herself, while Merlin just stands there and laughs at her like he agrees but it doesn't matter.

I like the word "skunked." It has a nice ring to it that can evoke a response from all five senses. For instance, I was "skunked" in the rotten egg fight – forty-two to nothing. Mom says I smelled worse than a skunk. That isn't what it means though. I lost so bad that I didn't score a single point. Getting skunked is generally disgraceful unless you laugh about it like you weren't really trying as hard as you could.

If somebody runs over a skunk on the road, you will know about it for a long time if you drive by. You don't want to stop the car and park right there unless it is really important. It's like that when you get skunked in a game. You don't want to stop at that level of expertise or people will say you stink. You will notice most stuff because you see it or hear it or feel it, but you are most likely to notice a skunk because you smell it. Smell is a really neat sense that a lot of adults forget to enjoy. They get focused on avoiding bad smells like rotten food or bad breath. The smell of hot bread baking in the oven and flowers and puppy breath after they finish nursing and clean sheets on the bed should not be forgotten. I bet there are more good smells than there are bad ones. It's all a matter of what you pay attention to.

You are more likely to notice things you feel if you shut your eyes. Then you can't get your information by looking at it. Information you get by feeling something is not usually forgotten. I still remember how the cow's wet tail swatting me in the face feels. I don't have to be reminded to tuck my head in close to the cow's withers when I am reaching underneath. I bet it would feel good to hold Violet's hand, but I haven't dared try that yet. Guinevere shuts her eyes when she kisses King Arthur. She only does that when she thinks we aren't looking. I asked her why she does that and she got all red faced and said she doesn't know. I bet it feels better that way. I tried closing my eyes when I kissed Aunt Gertrude goodbye once, but I knocked her glasses off and it didn't work well.

I remind you of skunks and senses and stuff because you are about to hear a story of bravery beyond fighting dragons and wolves and lions. It is remarkable for not following any of the conventional wisdom. No physical risk is taken. We saw and felt the skunks without smelling them. We didn't even know how brave we were until adults told us all the bad things that could have happened. Not one adult I have ever talked to would take the same risks. Like I pointed out earlier, most adults spend too much effort avoiding bad smells to allow for the fun they could have.

I asked Merlin why we hardly ever see a skunk that hasn't been run over. He says they usually hunt food at night when we are in the house. Pictures of skunks are pretty with dark black body and white stripe from their head all the way to the end of their tail. Some people have skunks that are descented as pets. Makes you wonder what the doctor who descents skunks smells like. Mom says some perfume is made with skunk oil as its base. That's hard to figure out. Maybe people who don't like other people wear that perfume to keep others away.

I saw a skunk behind the machine shed one afternoon while I was sitting on the ground near the sand box. Everyone in the sand box prison was busy road building, so I decided to watch the skunk. It was poking its nose into every clump of grass and under little bits of scrap wood. I know better than to chase a skunk.

Merlin tells a funny story of trying to chase a skunk out of the barn. He opened the barn door so it could easily get away. The skunk just kept poking around in front of the stalls getting a bite of oats the cows missed. He threw some stuff in the general direction of the skunk and it faced him and dared him to get closer and then kept rummaging around for spilled oats. A chicken perched on the manger saw the oats the skunk found under some straw. The chicken decided to fly down and get a few of the oats. The skunk decided the chicken was attacking so he let loose with a stink bomb and then ran out the open door.

Merlin said the chicken ran in circles squawking before it escaped out the open door as well. Merlin didn't think he was close enough to get much of the smell on him. Mom made him take a robe to the woodshed and scrub with two quarts of canned tomatoes before he came into the house to get a bath. He left his clothes soaking in the lake in a gunnysack with some lye soap. They still smelled so bad a week later that he buried his pants and shirt. The barn smelled bad for a month.

I climb up on the machine shop roof and walk over to the corner nearest the skunk and watch him. He pays no attention to me as he hunts grubs. Skunks don't move

102

very fast. This skunk waddles around a while, and then he heads straight toward a big stump. I watch the whole thing from my perch on the corner of the machine shed. The skunk disappears into a hole at the base of the stump and doesn't come back out.

I get tired of watching the stump after a while so I go back to the sand box prison to report my findings. I imagine the skunk went into his den to take a nap. I name him Otto because he walks funny like old man Otto. I wonder if he is the same skunk that Merlin tangled with.

I lead an expedition to the stump after breakfast the next day. I am a long way in the lead because my armor bearers have heard Merlin's skunk story as well, and they're chickens. (That's a joke. Merlin would have been better off if his chicken hadn't been so brave.) I got a different message from Merlin's story. The skunk didn't mind him being around until the stupid chicken tried to get his oats. I figure skunks won't bother you unless you bother them. We walk around the stump studying it from a distance. No one wants to get too close, including me. I figure the best way to get a look at the skunk is to lure him out of his den. I send the armor bearers to the corn crib to get an ear of corn.

I sit on the ground about twenty feet from the stump and watch the opening to the skunk's house. I think I see something inside, but it is really hard to be sure. A black animal in a black hole is hard to see. The armor bearers bring the ear of corn, keeping me between them and the stump.

They ask, "Did you see the skunk?"

I say, "I think so, but I'm not sure."

They ask, "Are you going to throw the corn ear at the stump?" They want a warning before I do that because they are going to run for the house if I do.

I tell them, "Sit quietly and watch. I will lure the skunk out so we can see what he will do."

I shell the corn kernels from the cob. I gently toss the kernels about half way to the stump. We settle in, waiting for the bait to lure the skunk out. The sun is warm and nothing is happening. Two of the armor bearers fall asleep and the rest are huddled around an ant hill when mom calls us in for dinner. They are tormenting the ants by dropping a few grains of sand in their holes and watching the aunts clear the tunnels. The ants drag a grasshopper leg to their hole and are trying to haul it down the hole, but it won't fit.

We reluctantly go in for dinner with no certain evidence the skunk is even in the den. Later in the afternoon, I return to check the skunk hole while the rest are back to work creating a different set of roads in the sand box. There is no skunk to be seen, but most of the corn is gone. I imagine some chickens might have found it, but they don't eat the whole corn kernels well unless they are cracked. I also figure a chicken wouldn't leave a handful of corn until every last kernel is gone. I think the skunk helped himself while we were having dinner and getting naps. My report is greeted with skepticism at the sand box, but we plan another trip to the skunk den in the morning. We will bring corn with us this time.

The next day the armor bearers are braver since they are beginning to think the skunk is imaginary. I am offended by that implication, especially since they always listen to my stories with awe and never question any detail no matter how unlikely. We walk much closer to the stump as we circle it trying to see into the skunk hole. All of yesterday's corn is gone. We sit down within 10 feet of the opening to the skunk den and I shell another ear of corn. I toss each kernel as close to the den as I can. One kernel goes into the hole and I am sure something moved inside. We all get up and move back to a more respectable distance before sitting down to wait.

No skunk appears by dinner time. I check again later in the afternoon and find a lot of the corn gone. It is only after five ears of corn and nearly a week of waiting that our persistence is rewarded. The skunk pokes his head out of the hole and looks at us. He then gobbles up all the corn right at the door to the den and backs out of sight. I am exonerated. No one will ever doubt my stories again.

We sit patiently until dinner time without seeing the skunk again. The next morning two little skunks poke their heads out of the den and then just come right out into the grass and nibble on the corn. They are followed by four more little skunks, and then Mamma skunk puts her head out and watches her babies carefully.

We get up carefully to go in for dinner when it is time. We have not moved for over an hour partly out of wonder and partly out of fear of disturbing the skunk family. This afternoon we decide that each armor bearer can name one baby skunk since I have already named mamma skunk "Otto." Once you're named, you're stuck with the name even if people call you something else.

We can't tell the babies apart, but we still give them all names. We have no way of knowing if we are applying the names to the correct baby skunks, but then, who would know if we were wrong.

We are busy playing with our newfound friends a week later when we hear a scream. We thought Mom must have hurt herself, but she is running toward us with vigor. The baby skunks have learned to run out of the den as soon as we arrive and climb onto our laps to get the corn as we shell it. Otto stays at least three or four feet away from us as she eats some of the corn and keeps a close eye on her babies. I look at the two baby skunks crawling on my lap and at Otto who has turned to look at the approaching threat. I think about Merlin and the chicken and the skunk.

Mom can really mess us up if she keeps running toward us. I slowly stand up and face Mom who is already slowing way down. I hold my hands out, palms down, and say quietly: "We're OK! Don't upset Otto!"

Mom stops and looks around. She says, "Who's Otto?"

I reply, "Otto is the mamma skunk." I then recite the names of the six baby skunks and say they are Otto's family.

Mom very cautiously comes a bit closer. The whole skunk family can sense something isn't right and they all scurry back into their den. Mom had called us for dinner and we were so busy playing with the skunks that we didn't hear her. When she came to find out why we weren't coming in, she nearly got us skunked. That would have been none for us and one for the skunks. Now you have a better understanding of that term.

Two of the baby skunks have girl names and four have boy names. The adults want to know how we know which ones are boys and which ones are girls and why mamma skunk is named Otto. They seem more confused as we explain the whole situation. Getting adults mixed up in kid business can wreck everything. We are ordered to stay away from the skunks. We hear about rabies and lots of other scary things that happen to people who make friends with skunks.

I still throw an ear of corn over by the stump every afternoon, but I haven't seen Otto and her family since we were told we couldn't play with the skunks anymore. Mom may have told the skunks they couldn't play with us as well. I don't think she knows skunk talk. In fact, I've never heard a skunk say anything. They aren't great at threatening someone. They shoot first and ask questions later. No one is still hanging around to hear the questions. Maybe Merlin had something to do with ordering the skunks away. It seems like he would have used his influence earlier if he was that good. You want to try real hard not to get skunked

EENY INY OVER

A knight of any stature learns that collective action trumps individual effort. Sir Lancelot quickly learned to include others in his adventure tales. Their involvement ensures their interest in those tales. Most of the toys enjoyed on the farm are manufactured for adult use and recycled as toys when the adults have used them up. Each of us is given an allowance of one penny weekly. We are taught to give ten percent of our earnings to someone less fortunate than ourselves. It is hard to remember when you last put a penny in the Sunday school offering when that only happens once every ten weeks. I don't know why we always figure God is less fortunate than us. I understand He was treated pretty mean when He came to help us out a long time ago.

We don't have any concept of saving for retirement and such, so most of the pennies are spent at the next trip to the co-op where a penny will buy a stick of lickerish or several pieces of hard candy. I noticed the finest ball ever at Woolworths in Superior. It was solid rubber and had swirls of any color you can imagine all over it. It will bounce really high if you throw it down on a hard tile floor like the one at Woolworths. The clerks don't like you to do that because the ball can land on a shelf a long way off and knock something over. The ball costs twenty nine cents. Merlin explained that was over a half year of allowance when I checked on the possibility of a small advance. He observed that all seven of us can pool our allowances and buy the ball in five weeks and we will have enough left over for one piece of candy each and ten percent for God.

A plan is hatched on the spot. We will all put our allowances into a jar in the kitchen for the next five weeks. When the jar has accumulated enough money, Merlin will pick up the multicolored rubber ball at Woolworths. We will jointly own the new ball and play lots of games with it. The plan nearly disintegrates two weeks later when the youngest armor bearer wants to withdraw from the pact and purchase candy. I offer to give him my piece of candy when the ball is purchased and the plan stays intact. We can tolerate one defection, but the dam might break if one breach is allowed. It takes a lot of work to keep a coalition together for such a long time, but the prize is worth the effort. Not one day passes for five weeks without discussion of rules for various ball games. New games are invented daily. Bounce ball, catch, ball in the hole, ball tag, keep away, competitive catching, and eeny iny over.

We will bounce the ball off the wall of the barn and see who can catch it most often. We will toss the ball between two players while the others try to snatch it out of the air. We will toss the ball from one to another attempting to never miss a catch. We will toss the ball into a box with a hole cut in it. We will toss the ball onto the roof of the machine shed and try to catch it as it rolls down the sloping roof. I will throw the ball over the sand box prison wall and all inside will attempt to catch it. The catcher will throw the ball back out to me and be allowed to choose whichever digging tool he prefers. We will have a team at the front of the house and at the back of the house to throw the ball over the house roof. A judge will run back and forth to see if the receiving team catches the ball. The throwing team will warn of the ball on the way by shouting "EENY INY OVER". If the ball doesn't make it over the roof, the throwing team will shout "PIG TAILS" and must catch the ball before it hits the ground on their side. We will take turns sleeping with the ball, and the one who sleeps with the ball will choose the first game to be played the next day.

The ball is such an obsession with the entire group that it will have to end in disappointment. Nothing short of Heaven can be that good.

The fifth week has passed and Merlin returns from Superior with some farm supplies and the prettiest multicolored rubber ball you ever saw. It is late in the day, and I and each of the armor bearers look the ball over carefully and bounce it on the cement porch floor. We have to come in for supper and learn a new rule. We cannot throw the ball in the house. I get to sleep with the ball the first night because it was my idea to purchase the ball with our pooled funds. I am the first one in bed tonight in an unusual turnabout since the youngest one is usually tucked in first. My brother and oldest cousin and I sleep together in one bed. We lay awake for a long time discussing which game should be played first. I remind them that the final choice is mine, but I am open to suggestions.

I awaken early. I vaguely remember King Arthur and Merlin getting up to start chores, but I must have fallen back asleep. I reach under my pillow for the ball. I panic! I jump to my feet in the middle of the bed and awaking my groggy bed mates! The ball is gone! We all jump out of bed and jerk the covers off! The ball isn't there! We look under the bed and find only dust devils. That reminds me of Merlin's joke.

He said "From dust we are made and to dust we will return. There's someone under my bed, and I don't know if he's coming or going." I'll bet you can't forget that joke for the rest of your life no matter how hard you try. We are about to alert the entire kingdom about the vanishing ball when the ball is discovered in a dark corner under the dresser.

Mom isn't as excited about the ball games as we are. After breakfast, she says "You have to collect the outside eggs before you take the ball out to play."

I think we skipped a few nests in our haste. Now it is time to announce the first game. I think I settled on one before going to sleep, but we talked about all of the games and their rules last night. I must have fallen asleep without a firm decision. Now it's harder than ever because everyone is shouting the name of a different game, some of which haven't even been invented yet.

I draw my sword and hold it high until order prevails. We will vote. Votes are cast with raised hands. The first game will be "catch". Anyone who misses the ball thrown to them will drop out until only one is left. The winner gets to select the next game.

Mom has to call us three times for dinner. We put the ball in a box in the entry way where we have decided to store it when it isn't in use. It's hard to imagine that ball won't always be in use unless we're eating or in church or something. This is the first big purchase we have ever made and it is even more important because we planned and waited and dreamed. The sand box prison is slated for the afternoon after naps. The only game compatible with prison is for me to toss the ball over the fence and see who can catch it in order to select his excavation equipment. After the fourth throw over the fence, my armor bearers decide they can play catch inside the prison and my participation is unnecessary. I debate climbing back inside so I can participate. When I ask them to toss the ball back to me they said I can come in and play with them inside.

I am faced with a terrible moral dilemma. I can give up my unique freedom to join the crowd or face the lonely life of the rebel. It is a close call. I could say I was free within the prison if I had the power to escape at will. I fell asleep pondering that dilemma under the oak tree. I stayed awake a long time last night deciding how to play ball today and my fatigue protected me from the tempting mistake. The last time I joined the crowd in order to be near Violet, it hadn't turned out well. I awakened to come in for supper.

The dinner table talk was all about the games we played that day, with each claiming superior skills. Mom solved the problem of who should sleep with the ball tonight and forever after by suggesting we write our names on a paper in alphabetical order. That would be the order in which the ball would be assigned for each night. Amy was first and would sleep with the ball tonight. Sir Lancelot was last so it would be fair as I have already had my night with the ball.

I hoped we could vote for the first game tomorrow morning, but Amy was next to youngest and a girl. She enjoyed her unaccustomed position of authority a bit too much. She not only said she would make the game choice without consultation, she would not give us any hint of the game she would choose until after breakfast.

Yesterday, we enjoyed every game we played, but ball tag was the most fun. If you threw the ball at someone and it missed, you had to get the ball while everyone ran away. We would then taunt the thrower by getting close while ready to dodge the ball. Amy surprised us all. She chose eeny iny over. She is too small to throw the ball over the roof of the house. We never got to that game yesterday.

She had a motive to her madness. This is a team game and she hadn't fared so well at the games of individual skill. She picked me and my older brother as her teammates. This is an awesome team and is likely to prevail in this difficult game. An umpire is chosen and the remaining three are the opposing team. We start with the ball, and Alice shouts "EENY INY OVER" and throws the ball at the house roof with all of her might. The ball hits nearly halfway up the roof and bounces back toward us. I shout "Pig tails" before my brother catches the rebound. He then shouts "EENY INY OVER" and launches the ball in a great arc over the house. It is not caught and we are up one point. The game continues on and on with us leading the whole time. We are up over ten points when disaster strikes.

The ball just makes it over the peak of the roof and rolls toward us for an easy catch. The ball rolls into the drain gutter at the roof edge and stays right there. The other team and the umpire come around the corner of the house to see what is wrong. We can just catch a glimpse of the top of the ball in the rain gutter. We point out the problem. The thrower is first blamed and then exonerated. Alice takes heat for selecting this game in the first place. We throw sticks and stones at the ball. It will not be dislodged in that fashion. We hunt a long branch with which to knock the ball out of the gutter. None is even close to long enough including a branch so heavy that two of us are required to elevate it toward the gutter.

Don't forget that I am Sir Lancelot, pledged to protect the Kingdom from all danger and insult. I have special responsibility to rescue our ball from the evil rain gutter. I have a bit of roof experience. Remember the time I saved the calf from a pack of wolves? I will climb out onto the porch roof and climb up to where it joins the house roof. It will then be easy to walk up over the peak of the roof and get the ball out of the rain gutter. I will then retrace my steps back into the bedroom and we will play a different ball game.

Mom will not sanction the plan so we have to find a way around that obstacle. She still doesn't know I can get out onto the porch roof. Everyone has assumed the porch drain pipe was knocked loose by the wind. Our plan is to go into the house for a drink of water. We will all come in and go out several times so Mom loses track of who is and who isn't in the house. Then I will sneak upstairs to our bedroom and execute the ball rescue.

It is really hard to pretend something isn't up when something is up. Mom is quickly suspicious of our odd behavior. She asks Amy what is going on. Amy tries to cover my tracks with a lie, but she's not good at it. She says, "Sir Lancelot isn't in the house." Then, feeling guilty about her lie, she recants and says, "Sir Lancelot might be in the house, but he is going out to get the

114

ball." Mom is puzzled, but the significance of the last statement escapes her.

The plan is ingenious. I am in my bedroom undetected. The window is cracked open enough for me to squeeze out onto the porch roof. This time I head uphill to where the porch roof merges with the steeper house roof. As I transition to the house roof, I realize the slope is a lot steeper here. I never noticed that before. I can walk upright on the porch roof. I can only proceed up toward the peak of the house roof on my hands and knees. I slip backwards a bit as I crawl up the roof. My heart is pounding. I am a lot higher than I can ever remember being. If I slide down on this side, I will be able to stop when I reach the porch roof. Once over the peak, I will have nothing to stop me if I start sliding down.

I have heard warnings that it might break my neck if I fall many times in days gone by. These warnings never seemed credible as they were given when I was walking on the top board of a board fence or climbing an apple tree close to the ground. I flex my neck and turn my head at the top of the house roof. I'm trying to assess if my neck is likely to break if I fall. I decide that the ball rescue makes that risk worthwhile. Remember, bravery isn't absence of fear. Bravery is exhibited when one proceeds in the presence of fear. Sir Lancelot is brave and afraid. He might even be crazy since he is the only Johnson who has ever been sent to a psychiatrist. He knows his duty and is going to do it.

Mom knows something is afoot when she sees everyone except Sir Lancelot standing in the front yard in a tight group looking up at the house roof. She walks out the front door to the group of kids and turns to see what they are looking at. Sir Lancelot is sliding down the roof of the house. She puts her hands to her head and screams "What are you doing?" I am afraid of falling off the roof, but that is nothing to the fear that grips my heart as I find I am discovered where I don't belong. My pants are climbing up my leg as I slowly crawl toward the edge of the roof. I shout, "I am just getting the ball out of the rain gutter."

Mom shouts, "Get down from there!" She then corrects herself and shouts, "Be careful!" Those are reassuring words. Mom isn't mad, she's just concerned.

I put one foot in the gutter and the sliding tendency is stopped. I skillfully kick the ball out of the gutter with my other foot to the cheers of the audience. I then scramble up over the top of the roof and into the bedroom window. Mom rushes around to the other side of the house to see what's happening, but I am back inside my bedroom before she can see where I am. I run down the stairs and out the front door where the armor bearers are playing catch with the ball. Mom comes around the house, and everything is back to normal.

Mom wonders if she is hallucinating. She asks "What were you doing on the roof?

I explain "The ball got stuck and I just got it down." She doesn't ask how I got on the roof. This kid will probably tell her he can fly.

She simply states "You are not to get on the roof again!" Who would think that was a necessary instruction to give a five year old even if he seems to be part monkey?

HIDE AND SEEK

Sir Lancelot, like all of the King's court, finds recreation necessary to fill moments between dangerous adventures. As you might guess, a knight of Sir Lancelot's stature might find danger and adventure in places others would expect only peace and calm. I am convinced that most conflict is the result of misunderstandings and unrealistic expectations rather than perfidious intentions. Therefore, I stood on the kitchen porch with my great notched sword held high in the air. The gesture and stance command respect and attention. No one has ever explained that fact to the armor bearers. It is just a fact which has never been challenged. No one has ever loudly demanded attention or quiet when the sword is held high. The gesture itself demands that response.

A morning of recreation is about to begin now that the eggs are collected, chickens fed, and breakfast behind us. We all know that imprisonment in the sand box will follow after lunch and naps. Now is the time for games and fun. I am reviewing the rules for our version of the age old game of "hide and seek". This game may seem simple to the uninitiated, but there are many possible points of conflict and disagreement if the rules are not clearly understood by all participants. No standardized set of rules like "Robert's Rules of Order" can be referenced should disagreement arise during the course of the game. I am not a tyrant, dictating rules to subservient subjects. I merely raise each point of order and restate the final group consensus on each. The game is always more fun when it is played in a manner acceptable to each player.

The general format of the game is as follows:
1. Boundaries are identified within which the game is played.
2. The first seeker is chosen by drawing straws – shortest wins.
3. The seeker counts to a specified number with his head against the goal so he cannot see where players are hiding.
4. The seeker counts loudly so hiders know how much time they have left to get hidden.
5. The seeker must loudly holler out "Ready or not, here I come!" prior to opening his eyes to look for hidden players.
6. If the seeker finds a hider, he must tag the hider before the hider is able to touch the goal and become immune.
7. Once tagged prior to gaining immunity a player then aids the seeker in this search and may tag found hiders as well.
8. Immune hiders who touch the goal prior to being tagged are allowed to verbally harass the seeker and tagged hiders for any supposed ineptitude or lack of any desirable quality until the last hider is discovered at which time all insulting comments loose their validity and everyone is again equal.

9. The next seeker is chosen by straw selection from those who are immune. If no one made the goal untagged, all are included in the candidate pool as next seeker except the last seeker.
10. No score is kept. Each round is a complete episode. There are no hide and seek trophies to be won.

I open the discussion with suggestions for boundaries of the playing field. This is the most contentious subject which has only one proponent for each suggestion. We narrow down the choices by eliminating broad categories. We arrive at a final choice of one set of boundaries. The barn and farmhouse are rejected. This beautiful sunny day needs to be enjoyed outside. The pasture has too many uncured cow pies and is eliminated. The yard and outbuildings are rejected as having so many hiding places that one game round may never be completed. The woods are eliminated as they are out of bounds for our play area without special permission. The alfalfa field is eliminated because the plants will catch your ankles and trip you if you run in it and the plants are not tall enough to be good hiding places. The final consensus was hailed by all as the best choice. We will play the game in the sorghum grass field next to the pasture. There is a fence around it so the boundaries are easily established. The grass is nearly as tall as the participants, so hiding is possible anywhere within the field. No one can hide forever delaying the game because the bent grass trail can be followed to discover any well hidden participant. Ten acres offers enough hiding territory to keep seekers working.

Perfect! Now how high should the count proceed before calling out "Ready or not". The decision was bifurcated. The two smallest armor bearers only have to count to 10 and the rest have to count to 100. The goal is quickly selected as the corner fence post closest to the barn. Six straws are quickly prepared by cutting six equal and one short stem of sorghum grass.

I hold the straws in my hand with each projecting equally and each armor bearer selects one. The third draw is the sort straw and selection of the first seeker is over. I would have been recipient of the last straw if no one had selected the short straw.

The Kingdom of Johnson is known far and wide as a place where fair play is honored. The only exception I can recall is the egg fight which no one would say was fair play. The initial plan eliminated me from danger and the outcome subjected me only to the danger. I guess there is a poetic justice in even that outcome.

Hide and seek is a great game as it allows players of varying athletic and other skills to compete with opponents with different skill sets. One strategy is to hide near the goal and leap up to gain immunity when the seeker moves too far from the goal in search of hiders. Another strategy is to hide far from the goal where the seeker will be reluctant to follow as he must leave the goal untended for others to reach. I am a fast runner and think it would be wise to hide far from the goal so I can dodge the seeker and outrace him to the safety of the goal post.

The first round of the game surprised me. The seeker tagged the two youngest players immediately. He then assigned them to guard the goal post as he ranged further away and flushed two more hiders, one of whom was tagged by the goal post guards. I was then tracked down by the seeker and chased all over the field until I was finally tagged by a goal guard as I tried to gain immunity. The one immune player called out the most outrageous criticisms of my intellect and athletic ability the entire time. It's worth getting tagged just to stop the harassment. We can hardly get the next round going because everyone is rolling around in the grass laughing at how badly I had been harassed. There is nothing to be done but to join in the laughter because my own rule on harassing requires no retaliation if it is done according to the rules.

No straws need to be drawn to select the next seeker. Only one hider has gained immunity at the goal post. The count is going to be 100 again so I have a lot of time to consider my hiding strategy. It will be harder to track hiders as the last round created a lot of trails through the tall grass. I decide to run straight out for a long way and then circle back closer to the goal so I can leap up and run to the goal when the seeker follows my trail past my hiding place. Crouching down low is all that is required to hide in the tall grass. I have run most of the way across the field and am half way back as the seeker calls out "Ready or not!" I dive forward into the tall grass.

I immediately feel a searing hot pain in my right hand and hear a loud buzzing around my head. Two more painful stings to my cheek and neck occur as I realize I have punctured a hornet's nest with my great notched sword. I leap to my feet and race toward the goal which is next to the gate. The seeker runs toward me to block my path to the goal. Two hiders near the goal leap up and gain immunity. I am running in a peculiar way spinning around and swinging my sword frantically. The seeker slows as I approach fearing I am trying to escape being tagged by scaring him with my sword and shouting "Run!" He follows my instruction to run when I shout "Hornets!"

A hornet sting to his left arm speeds up his run considerably. None of the immune hiders even thinks of harassing me this time. They sense the urgency of our flight and push the gate open and run for the house ahead of us. We burst through the kitchen door and collapse in a heap on the kitchen floor.

Guinevere springs into action, grabbing a flyswatter to dispatch the few hornets that followed us all the way to the house. The smallest armor bearer is still walking to the house, crying. He has a sting over his right eye and it is swelling shut. He got too tired to run and lagged behind. The hornets seemed to be after me primarily. All of us have at least one sting. I have whelps all over my face and arms and neck. I whacked a few of my attackers with my great notched sword but there were far too many to be warded off.

We all shed our T shirts and Guinevere puts a drop of mercuricomb iodine on each sting. This stuff stings nearly as badly as a hornet sting. She then makes a paste of baking soda and water. As she dobs the paste on the stings, the stinging sensation is greatly reduced. I have over 20 stings while each of the others had one to 5 stings. I feel really sick and weak.

Guinevere continues her treatment by giving each of us an aspirin and a glass of water. She then puts a large pot of water on the stove, adding rolled oats when it begins to boil. She boils the thin oatmeal for fifteen minutes or so. She then sets the pot in a sink of cool water to cool off. When the oatmeal has cooled enough to allow her hands to tolerate the heat, she scoops out handfuls of oatmeal and covers all of the stings with gobs of oatmeal. The warm soothing mixture feels wonderful.

I don't remember anything after that until I wake up the next morning with a high fever, feeling very weak. Guinevere is placing cool cloths on my forehead. Merlin and King Arthur are there as well. King Arthur has the family Bible in his lap and I realized he has been praying for me. When I wake up Guinevere leans forward and kisses me on the forehead right where there is a gob of wet oatmeal. King Arthur and Merlin both leap up to hug me and thank God for me. They both kiss me several times getting oatmeal all over the sheets and their own faces. It is really embarrassing for a Knight to be kissed by the King and Queen and Magician. I think a speech or soliloquy or such would be more dignified.

I ask, "What is going on?"

Guinevere said, "You were stung by hornets."

I said, "I knew that before you did."

Everyone in the room laughs.

Merlin says, "Guinevere ran out to the cornfield where we were cultivating. She said you were dying."

All work stopped and Dr. Jensen was called. He said "It is too late for me to do anything as Sir Lancelot is already unconscious." He instructed King Arthur to keep my head tilted back and use a spoon to keep my airway open if I had trouble breathing. He suggested, "A shot of whiskey would be good if he can swallow." He then suggested aspirin every 4 hours, cool cloths and prayer. He arrived a few hours later and essentially repeated his advice and said, "The outcome is in God's hands." The others are nearly healed by the time Dr. Jensen arrived. He looked at each one and listened to their hearts and checked their temperatures. Only one had a low grade fever and the whelps at the sting sites were all nearly resolved.

Dr. Jensen supervised my swallow of a spoonful of Old Overholt and had a double shot himself. He slept on the couch and is asleep down there right now.

Merlin goes downstairs to get Dr. Jensen. They come in with great smiles on their faces. Dr. Jensen is wearing his dark suit which is all rumpled up. He slaps King Arthur on the back and says, "God was with you! I will be on my way as I am no longer needed."

Guinevere says, "You can't leave without breakfast!" She leads him downstairs. The smell of fried potatoes, bacon and eggs wafts up the stairs. The rest of

124

us realize we are hungry and head downstairs for breakfast after I slip on my Jeans and T shirt. I am surprised to find my legs feel weak even though I am recovered from the Hornet stings.

I organize a meeting of the Round table where we will memorialize the events of that fateful game of hide and seek. The Armor bearers show each place where they had been stung.

I explain "I attacked the hornets when I realized they were endangering the entire Kingdom of Johnson. " I ask Merlin, "What more should be done to protect against these dangerous insects."

Merlin said, "I found the hornets nest late last night when they were inactive and poured gasoline on the nest and ignited it. They will be more careful about who they sting next time."

We discussed whether the great notched sword should have one or twenty more notches to commemorate my most dangerous adventure. Merlin said one notch would be best but it is twenty times more important than any of the others.

I WAS WRONG ABOUT GIRLS

I was in love once. I learned that dreams of love are not matched by reality. After Violet's visit, I made it a point to huddle with interested groups of guys after church and tell them tales of heroism. They appreciate my bravery even more when I admit I am afraid at times. They understand that foolhardiness is not an example of bravery.

I keep an eye on the girls including my cousins who are likely to braid weeds into ornaments and compare clothes and a lot of other girl stuff. Violet is there every Sunday, but we never speak. I am polite enough with a nod of the head to acknowledge her presence. I am not about to approach her in such a way that I can be rebuffed and thus humiliated. I kind of wish I hadn't done the poison frog thing when she didn't climb out of the sand box prison. I am willing to say I'm sorry, but that might expose me to the rebuff I fear. It's hard to get an apology together when you're not even sure you're sorry you did something. It's equally hard to ask someone to apologize for ruining your dreams when they didn't even know what your dreams were.

Mom and the Iversons seem to have a lot to talk about today. Violet is brought into the conversation and claps her hands and jumps up and down over something they are talking about. I have to be careful so no one notices my interest in the matter. I go on with my description of the rotten egg fight. All the guys are rolling on the ground laughing at how I was waylaid by my own troops. They think it is the greatest joke ever. I explain, "I was humiliated even more when I had to strip down on the porch before coming into the house to get cleaned up." They are astonished at my answer when they ask how I got even.

I tell them, "It is impossible to think of any response that could even that score, so I just chalked it up to experience. In fact, I think it was a pretty good joke too. They needed a target and no one can handle adversity better than me."

I still leave room for retaliation if they try anything like that again. People don't like you if you have to win every time. I win a few. I lose a few. I still forge ahead. Tag is no fun if you're always "it".

In the car, mom tells us "Violet is leaving the Iversons next week. I invited them over to visit again next Thursday before Violet leaves to go home for school. Violet's parents are returning from their mission trip and will pick her up after church next Sunday."

I exhibit no expression of interest other than to state "Maybe we can have a picnic."

I need to be really cool so I won't be suspected of having too much interest. The last visit was so disappointing that another couldn't be worse. I'm not going to try to get her attention with another frog. I have to confess that I think of her last visit often and see many places where I made mistakes. I probably scared her by being too interested in her even though I hid it pretty good. Why should I expect her to climb out of the sand box when even my older brother won't do it? What made me scare everyone with the frog? I'm a lot more mature now.

Everyone in the car agrees that a picnic is a great way to spend our day Thursday. I put forward a lot of ideas.

"We can go to the roadside table at Solen Springs. We can start early in the day so we can have our picnic at noon. We can all make our own sandwiches with bought bread. We can walk to the pond just past the lane in the woods."

All of my suggestions lead away from the sand box. I don't think anyone notices.

The girls say "We can play ball tag." All of the armor bearers sense an adventure developing. I wonder if Violet will bring a scarf she can leave with me in case I have to risk my life while she is gone.

I ask "Do you think she might be visiting the Iversons again later on?" I realize I am getting way too enthusiastic about Violet's visit when Merlin turns around and looks at me.

He says, "You really like that girl, don't you?"

I said, "Naw, I just think picnics are a lot of fun."

Merlin grins a bit too much before he turns forward to watch the road again. I wonder if Wizards can read your mind. Merlin sure is hard to keep secrets from. He can be trusted to not blab them around so it's ok.

We have three days to plan for Thursday. I have so many plans that we will have to make this a two day visit. I spend all Monday morning in the kitchen suggesting additional details for the Thursday picnic. Mom tells me to go out and play with the others, but I want to be sure we have everything ready. Merlin comes up with the best plan of all after supper Monday night.

He says "We will load the wagon with hay and pull it out to the pond in the woods with the tractor."

He and King Arthur will load the hay wagon and park it near the kitchen door so Guinevere can load all the blankets to put on the ground and carry all the supplies for the picnic on the wagon. I think I will sit near violet so I can bump into her when the wagon goes over a rock or hump in the lane. I really don't know why I want to bump into her, but it makes my heart race to think about it. I will be sure it doesn't look like I did it on purpose.

I haven't been out to the pond since I got lost in the magic forest. I am sure Merlin will be able to prevent any magic being used against us. I want you to know I am not afraid to go back to the pond, but I am glad we are going as a group. Last time I came to the pond, I was alone, hunting a rogue dragon that had knocked the fence down and let the cows out.

This time the dragon is not a factor since he knows I will not allow him back in the Kingdom of Johnson. I will point out the scorched tree where the dragon has been. Most of the dragon tracks will probably be gone by now, but I will point out where they were.

Merlin loads slab wood for a fire on the back of the wagon and piles it high with hay to cushion our ride to the woods. He has the wagon parked next to the kitchen Tuesday afternoon. Mom piles a bunch of quilts on the hay. I help her since the picnic is my idea in the first place. I plan where everyone should sit, but Mom says we can all pile on and sit anywhere we like. I think it is just as well that I casually find a spot near Violet instead of making it look like I planned for this to happen.

I ask Merlin "Can we can ride around on the hay wagon a while instead of driving straight to the pond?"

He says "That's exactly what I plan to do!"

Wednesday lasts for as least a week. No one is locked in the sandbox so everyone can help decide what needs to be put on the hay wagon. Mom fries three chickens and wraps them in brown paper and towels and puts them in a wooden crate. She makes a big bowl of potato salad and puts it on ice in another box. She boils eggs and cuts them in half and digs out the yolks. She mixes the yolks up with pickles and mayonnaise and onions and puts the stuff back in the place where the yolk used to be. These are called deviled eggs and are really good. A 10 gallon milk can is filled with water and tied to the fender of the tractor so we will have plenty to drink. Mom says she plans to bring sugar and Kool-Aid. Glasses are stacked together with paper between them so they won't break. This will be the best picnic there ever was.

Wednesday night I request a meeting of the round table. I have a brilliant idea. This will be no ordinary picnic!

I explain "This event will be known as 'Violet's Farewell Feast'. We will make this an annual event to be celebrated for as long as the Kingdom of Johnson exists. We will all wear our royal clothing, and we will crown Violet as a Princess. We will have to make a suitable crown for her coronation."

Merlin says "This is exactly what is needed to complete planning for tomorrow's event. I will make the required crown." He notes that his wizard hat is getting a bit worn, and he will replace that as well. The magic scepter is in good condition and my notched sword is ready for action.

King Arthur and Guinevere aren't wearing their royal robes and crowns tonight, but they promise to wear them at "Violet's Farewell Feast".

Thursday morning, we collect the outside eggs. Merlin and King Arthur hook the hay wagon to the tractor after finishing chores. We have oatmeal with raisins and milk for breakfast. All of the big people have eggs and bacon and toast as well. My stomach is churning, and I think I might be getting sick.

Mom asks "Why don't you finish your cereal?"

I tell her, "I'm not very hungry."

I'm not going to spoil "Violet's Farewell Feast" by getting sick. I go into the bathroom and throw up. I feel fine after that. I don't let anyone know what happened. I'm not sure what happened myself.

The food is placed on the wagon and everything is checked to be sure nothing is forgotten. Two double bladed axes and a Swede saw are strapped to the tractor fender. Merlin says he will cut some branches for the big people to sit on. He brings some paper and matches to start a fire. We climb on and off the wagon rearranging the hay for our cushions until we hear a car coming up the driveway.

It's the Iversons and Violet. Our adventure is about to begin! Mom and Mrs. Iverson tell the girls they should go to the bathroom before we start out. That's the advantage of being a boy on the farm. Any tree or building or bush or whatever can be used as a urinal as long as no one sees you doing it. We sometimes line up on the side porch and have a contest to see who can pee the farthest. I'm not sure Mom would approve of that contest so we don't talk about it except among ourselves. We don't let the girls watch, but we do tell them who can pee the farthest. I can win sometimes if I drink a lot of water.

Mom and Mrs. Iverson get on the wagon near the back and lean against the hay piled on the slab wood. King Arthur and Mr. Iverson sit on the front of the wagon with their legs hanging over the edge. Merlin climbs onto the tractor and starts the engine. The eight remaining participants pile into the hay in the middle of the wagon. Everyone starts wrestling and jockeying for position and throwing hay and hollering. Merlin puts on his cone shaped magic cap and holds his scepter high. The new cap is taller than his old one and makes him look really important.

When a semblance of order is obtained, I find myself lying in the hay with my foot on top of Violet's leg. I hold my breath wondering when she will discover the intrusion. She doesn't push me away like I expect. I casually move to a more comfortable position and hold the great notched sword in the air.

King Arthur pulls on his Royal Robe and puts on his crown. He bellows out, "Let the celebration of 'Violet's Farewell Feast' begin!"

Merlin lets the clutch out on the tractor and the wagon lurches forward. He shouts "Geronimo!" even though he isn't jumping off anything.

Violet falls sideways right on top of me. I catch her so she won't be hurt. She laughs and says, "This is fun!"

I am at a complete loss of words for the first time I can remember. I just smile and hang on so she won't be hurt by the bouncing wagon.

Violet gets back up, sitting near me. I would like to reach out and hold her hand, but I know there are a lot of eyes on this wagon and I could be teased a long time if someone saw that happen. I get to my feet and raise my sword again. I point out where the dragon broke the fence. I point to the tree scorched by dragon breath. I point out the place where we planned our cattle drive. I point out the woods where I scouted for Dragon sign. We ride all the way around the pasture fence and back to the lane and then out alongside the cornfield and then over a small hill toward the woods.

We top the second hill and there is the pond where I searched for dragon tracks. It was here that I fell asleep and the magic forest enveloped me so I couldn't find my way home. I have to say I would be afraid right now if I was here by myself. We ride around the pond three times before Merlin picks out the perfect picnic spot. The spot is right below the giant tree where I fell asleep the last time I was here.

The grass is thick and soft to sit on. The tree provides comfortable shade from the hot sun. The slab wood is unloaded and Merlin splits one piece into thin slivers for kindling wood. Everyone under six years old searches the hillside for rocks and we make a rock ring around the fire. Mom and Mrs. Iverson arrange the blankets on the ground so they are on grass and not getting dirty. We all explore around the pond while the adults finish setting up the picnic site. We throw sticks and rocks into the water causing turtles to slip off their perches and swim away. We try to spot them sticking their heads up to get a breath of air.

Alice has our rubber ball. She throws the ball at me and says "You're it!" as she runs away. I run to get the ball and throw it at my older brother. He dodges the ball, and I have to run and pick it up to throw it at a slower runner. This time I get him and he runs for the ball while I get away. It is fun to play ball tag in the woods because you can run near the person with the ball and then duck behind a tree so he can't hit you with it. We are so tired from running away from the ball thrower that we fall on the ground to rest which makes us an easy target. I flop onto the ground to rest, and Violet flops down next to me.

She says, "This is fun!" for the second time today.

I answer, "This is the most fun I've ever had!"

She asks "Does this beat all of your exciting adventures?"

I reply, "I have never had a more fun adventure including getting two ice cream cones and meeting a man named 'Happy' who isn't a dwarf."

She asks "How did you get to be a knight?"

I tell her the story of King Arthur knighting me and how Merlin was a magician but never told anyone until I pointed out my real name – Sir Lancelot. I tell her "You are to be crowned a princess this very day by the King himself."

I explain "This day has been named 'Violet's Farewell Feast' and will be celebrated for as long as the Kingdom of Johnson exists."

Violet asks "What does a princess have to do?"

I explain " A princess just has to look pretty and fall in love with a worthy knight. I tell her she already looks pretty so all she has to do is find the right knight."

She tells me "I only know one knight, but that would probably be enough."

She is just taking off a silk scarf to put around my neck when the ball hits me in the side, waking me up as the thrower shouts "You're it!" I look for Violet and see her talking to Merlin next to the fire.

We stay at the pond until it is time for evening chores to start. The fire is out. The wagon is loaded. We drive straight home. Princess Violet leaves with the Iversons.

This was the best day of my life!

SIR LANCELOT GOES TO SCHOOL

I slay dragons on a regular basis. No situation causes me more than momentary concern. I am Sir Lancelot, and I'm about to embark on an exciting adventure. I've been well prepared by my associates who have preceded me in the field. Guinevere (mom) assures me that I will enjoy myself and distinguish myself. My older brother (the oldest armor bearer) tells me it is really easy and he is going on to the next level having conquered the challenges I am about to face.

In fact, I receive a maximum of reassurance with a minimum of information. I am about to start school without the slightest hint of what that means other than the warning that I will be an ignorant failure if I avoid the process. My clothing has been selected for me and a paper sack with my lunch is thrust into my hand as I am hurried to the road where I will meet the bus. I have seen my brother get on the bus over the past year, but I have never been on a bus myself. I have no Idea how I will direct the bus to take me to school and, more importantly, how I will get the bus to return me to my driveway when school is over. Such matters will just have to work themselves out as the need arises. I wait for the bus with growing apprehension as I realize the need to manage bus riding is imminent.

My brother stands beside me exhibiting no fear. Sir Lancelot therefore demonstrates none of the turmoil building within. My brother is starting second grade and is an expert on bus riding, but I am a leader, not a follower. No information is exchanged as we wait for the bus. Sir Lancelot is known for his loquaciousness, but is remarkably quiet today. The decision is already made by the brave, apprehensive dragon slayer that he will board the bus first, demonstrating his primacy to the world at large. I'm beginning to view Sir Lancelot in the third person as I realize he may not survive this day. It's good to view a disaster from as great a distance as possible, and I feel a bit of distance from the dragon slayer might be the best position for me at the moment.

The gigantic yellow vehicle appears in the distance, and quick plans are formulated. I'll head for the back of the bus and see if someone closer to the driver takes responsibility for directing him to the school. I hope we all have a common destination as I have no idea which school I am headed for if there are several choices. I don't know what a school looks like, but I envision it as a building similar to the church since the first room there is called Sunday school. Maybe it will be the same place except we won't be wearing our good clothes. Good clothes and Sunday clothes are synonymous terms for regular clothes that are fresh from washing and ironing.

My clothes today are close since this is only the second time I've worn them since washing and ironing. The bus stops. The strangely hinged door opens as if by magic, revealing black rubber steps with a yellow line on the front edge. I would like to examine these features in more detail, but any hesitation would allow my older brother to board first and spoil my carefully laid plans. I quickly board the bus and head for the back seat. I can see this was an important strategy as several big kids are on the bus and must be impressed at my self assurance. I don't know how I would recover if they saw me following my big brother like an ordinary being. Sir Lancelot is alive and well and master of the situation.

The bus driver manipulates a complicated lever and the door closes. My brother settles down in the third seat beside someone he seems to know. They begin an animated conversation, and I know my presence is forgotten. I will be able to observe their behavior without acknowledging any subservience. The bus driver doesn't seem to need any direction as he works the pedals and gear shift lever and stops again and again at small groups of kids along the roadside. He skillfully manipulates the lever attached to the door from the middle of the bus allowing additional passengers aboard.

He turns down a side road and turns again. He pulls into a driveway and backs up and returns the way we came, but then he turns again leaving me with no idea how we can find our way home again. No one on the bus exhibits any concern but I am beginning to think we are lost. If we don't find the school, I will be destined to be an ignorant failure, as that is the fate of those who don't attend school. I am saved by the knowledge that Sir Lancelot never fails. A dragon would be a welcome sight right now because Sir Lancelot knows just what to do with dragons. One swing of his sword and the dragon is slain. He doesn't worry about what must be done with a slain dragon as the admiring crowds will dispose of the carcass.

A lot of the big kids seem to know each other and join others in seats ahead of me. I sit alone in the back seat hoping I will see someone I know, but that doesn't happen. Although everyone on the bus seems to be ignoring me, I am sure they are aware of my self-assured demeanor and are even a bit in awe of being on the same bus as Sir Lancelot.

A lump forms in my throat as I realize I have no control over the current situation and no plans for the future. The bus ride is managed, but what will happen when it ends? I furtively watch my brother who has not once glanced back to see if I am still on the bus. I can be the last off the bus when it finally arrives at school since I am sitting in the back seat. That couldn't be seen as a mark of weakness-- just the effect of logistics. Then I will again assert my status as Sir Lancelot, dragon slayer, while everyone waits for a leader to emerge.

The bus crosses a railroad track and turns down a dirt road next to the tracks. It stops though no one is standing by the roadside. The driver works his lever and the door opens. A lot of talking begins as the big kids at the front of the bus stand and gather their lunch bags and coats and push each other around and begin exiting the bus. This is really puzzling as no building seems nearby that looks anything like my vision of a school. There are no adults present who could be teachers. Maybe we're just being kicked off the bus in a strange place where we'll never be found again. I kept track of the bus turns for a while, but finally lost all track of the way home. Sir Lancelot is lost.

My brother and his friend have exited the bus. I need to have some connect with safety and look for him anxiously as I step off the bus. He must be in the crowd of big kids milling around near the bus. I am the smallest person in the crowd. No one seems to be looking to me for leadership so that monkey is off my back. I don't think Sir Lancelot got off the bus.

The bus door closes as if we are now rejected and the bus slowly grinds on down the road. I am totally alone in a crowd of big kids who simply ignore me. That's even worse than if they attacked me. My brother isn't anywhere to be seen. Sir Lancelot is gone. It is the worst moment of my life. I begin to cry. No one here knows Sir Lancelot so there is no need to protect his reputation.

I look up and notice the crowd is thinning out and the roughhousing is diminishing. It seems that a line of big kids is making its way up a long hill along a poorly defined dirt path toward a large building. Could that be the school house? What do they do to you in a school house? Are helpful adults present? Can I make it up that long hill?

My legs feel weak. I can hardly see as tears blur my vision. If I stay where I am, I will be alone in a strange place. I have to follow the line of big kids up the hill or be forever lost and alone. Better to throw myself on the mercy of strangers than expire here. As I make my way up the long hill, I cry less fervently. I can see that a door is open and the big kids are going in. I am the last bus passenger to enter the large building. I encounter an angel who shows me where to hang my coat and where to put my lunch bag and shows me a desk where I will spend the next two months learning that school is really fun.

My brother has a desk two rows over and three seats back with the other second graders. I have the front seat in the first row and discover that there will be another first grader in the first seat of the second row. She is frightened by the prospect of going to school and doesn't talk for several days. She nods her head when the teacher asks her questions, which proves she can hear, but I thought she was unable to talk for nearly a whole week. At recess I told my brother they put me in the front of the room so I could be an example of bravery for the entire schoolroom. Before lunch I was able to determine the bus would pick us up at the bottom of the hill after school.

I assert, " I claim the back seat of the bus so I can guard the others on the way home.

Sir Lancelot confidently boards the bus after his first day at school and marches to his claimed rear seat. All the way home he regales his fellow schoolmates with tales of fearless exploits. The performance is so convincing that no one remembers the little kid crying at the bus stop on arrival at school that morning. I'm not sure when the real Sir Lancelot got off the bus that first day of school.

YOU'RE NOT DEAD UNTIL YOU'RE DEAD

First grade is an exciting adventure! I've been at it for over a month and believe I have enough to think about for several years. We learned the names of colors and the alphabet and counting to 100 already. This is pretty easy stuff since I already knew it from pumping my older brother for information every day when he got home from school last year. We each received a book to take home to practice reading. The stories are just a few sentences long under a picture which fills most of the page. Dick and Jane and Spot. The dog will be running in the picture and the words will be: "Run Spot, run. See spot run. Go Spot. Go Spot, go." Etc.

This isn't the stuff that keeps you up at night thinking about the story. I am used to meaty stuff read to me by Merlin like: "Alice in Wonderland" , "King Arthur and the Knights of the Round Table", "Tom Sawyer", "Huckleberry Finn", and poetry and Shakespearean plays. Mom reads us Bible stories straight out of the King James Bible. She scoffs at the children's Bible Story books which skip the hard to understand words. She says we have to learn them sometime and this is as good a time as any. We read most of Dante's "Inferno", but that's pretty hard for a kid to absorb. I decide to impress Ms. Moran, our first grade teacher with a compliment.

I say "Thou art a comely lass!"

She nearly falls over laughing.

I ask, "Do you understand formal English? I can explain the meaning."

She only laughs harder.

I think teachers prefer less formal language. I don't think she ever heard of Shakespeare.

I ask, "Are you familiar with King Arthur and Sir Lancelot?"

She says, "I read those stories in College."

I tell her "I am the modern Sir Lancelot and live with King Arthur, Guinevere and Merlin."

She seems a bit surprised. She has me come to her desk when school is over and gives me a note for my mom.

I don't try to read the note because she wrote it in cursive and I can only read printed stuff. I ask mom what it is about and she says, "Your teacher thinks you might be crazy just like the social worker did last summer. Mom writes a two page letter to Ms. Moran explaining that I was evaluated by a genuine psychiatrist last summer and he is certain that I am not crazy. She thanks Ms. Moran for her concern and assures her that she isn't the first to jump to that conclusion. She ends her note with the same words Merlin and the psychiatrist used. "He'll be okay if you don't fence him in". I'm pretty sure she isn't talking about the sand box prison, but I really don't know what they're getting at.

I'm getting sidetracked here, but the reading bit is central to a life threatening event. Merlin gave me a poetry book. It looks like it would be hard to read, but it is just printed in small print and my eyes are as good as anyone's. Lots of the poets use made-up words and shortened words so the stuff will rhyme or have a particular rhythm. Merlin can read some poetry with such good rhythm that you could set it to music. I often have to ask what certain words mean, but Merlin seems to always know the answer. When I ask why the poet didn't just say it straight out, Merlin says poetic license allows him to say it any way he pleases. I plan to get a poetic license myself because it is fun to say things people have to think about before they get what you are saying. I plan to use a lot of poetic license if I get a chance to tell violet what I think about her.

It is hard to read a book of poetry like one would read our book about Dick and Jane and Spot, but the stuff poets talk about is a whole lot more fun to think about. You can open the book to nearly any page and just read one or two pages to get the whole thing. Most of the poems take less than a page of print. My favorite poet is Ogden Nash whose poems are sometimes only a few lines long and are really funny:

"The Hippopotamus"

> "Behold the hippopotamus!
> We laugh at how he looks to us,
> And yet in moments dank and grim,
> I wonder how we look to him.
>
> Peace, peace, thou hippopotamus!
> We really look all right to us,
> As you no doubt delight the eye
> Of other hippopotami. "

Another poem I love to quote is:

> "Big fleas have little fleas upon their backs to bite 'em.

144

And little fleas have lesser fleas, so on, ad infinitum."

His shortest poem is about fleas:

" Adam had 'em."

You might guess that I like reading Merlin's book better than my first reader. It is important to have good light when you are reading hard stuff in small print, so I found a perfect spot in the tool shed right under a window. King Arthur has a cardboard barrel about eighteen inches in diameter and four feet deep. We buy special vitamins and minerals in these shipping containers to mix with the cow feed once a week. They come with a complicated locking ring which can only be opened by a grown-up with a pliers and screwdriver. When the barrel is empty, it makes a perfect waste basket in the tool shed and in the barn.

I find it pleasant to sit on top of the barrel with my thighs and back supporting me so I can be right near the window light which is coming in from the west in the afternoon. I am perched on the waste barrel with Merlin's book in my lap when tragedy strikes!

The place where my shoulder blades press on the rim of the barrel and the place where my legs rest on the barrel get numb so I shift my position to move the pressure points higher on my back and lower on my legs to ease the discomfort. My buttocks slip a bit deeper into the barrel and I am again comfortable for a while. The poem I am trying to figure out has a lot of big words in it. I lean forward a bit and squint to make out the meaning of a big word.

THUMP!!!!!

I slide to the bottom of the barrel with my knees against my ears and my hands are sticking straight up higher than my toes. My buttocks hit the bottom of the barrel so hard it knocks the wind out of me. I can't breathe! I panic for a moment! My legs are cramped from being bent back so far. I realize I have only a moment to live before I die of asphyxiation.

Within a minute I discover I can breathe if I don't try to take a deep breath. I force the panic back and began tiny shallow breaths.

It's a myth that your life flashes through your mind when you are about to die. I am certain I will die at first, but all I think about is what people would think when they finally find me. I wonder if they will find me before I start to stink. No one will think to look in the trash barrel for me. They might look in the tool shed when I don't show up for supper, but who would think to look in the barrel? Will they try to find the villain who stuffed me in there? I sure hope no one will be blamed for my own foolish demise.

The pain in my legs fades into the background as circulation to my legs is cut off. I can move my wrists and fingers, but there is nothing within reach to grasp. The only other thing I can move is my head. I remember a story Merlin told of a man who jumped out of an airplane without a parachute. There was no room in the tail gun position for a parachute and the plane was crashing with the rest of the crew already bailed out. He

146

kicked out a side panel and leaped out of the plane. He tried to spread his jacket to slow his fall. He fell through the branches of a large tree breaking a lot of bones. He was captured by the Germans who then sent him home when they understood what had happened to him. Merlin said to never forget: "YOU'RE NOT DEAD UNTIL YOU ARE DEAD"

This is how Merlin's magic spell saved my life. I begin rocking my head back and forth as hard as I can. The barrel begins to rock a bit and I time my head rocking to build momentum. The barrel moves a bit and leans against a bench. I nearly give up, but I resume the rocking, now sideways because the back and forth movement is stopped by the bench. The barrel starts rocking again and suddenly goes over center, tipping on its side.

Tipping over hurts almost as bad as falling into the barrel in the first place. I find myself on my back and inch out of the barrel by wiggling my ankles and my shoulders. An inch worm doesn't wiggle any better than me when my life depends on it. This is my closest brush with death since falling through the ice or being thrown onto an electrified barbed wire fence by a scared cow or being lost in a magic forest or lost in a strange city or fighting dragons, lions and wolves. I guess death is no stranger to me now that I ponder those and many other events. I don't think God wants me yet because He has passed on a lot of easy chances to invite me to my Heavenly Home.

I go to the house for supper and decide not to include this story in my tales of heroism as I cannot imagine anything heroic about it.

Merlin asks "Where did you leave the poetry book?"

I go back to the tool shed to retrieve it and set the barrel right side up.

I tell Merlin, "I was deep in thought over a tough poem and forgot to bring the book in."

I'm afraid he won't let me use his book if he discovers how careless I was with it. I will finish reading it on the davenport near a lamp.

SUNDAY SCHOOL

Mrs. Iverson is a bit old to be teaching a Sunday school class of rowdy boys. Mrs. Knutson is the regular boy's teacher and has the youth and energy to keep order even on hot Sunday mornings when the boy's class gets a bit fidgety. Two years ago a decision was made to separate the Sunday school classes into three groups: 1) Adults. 2) Boys. 3) Girls. The earlier attempt to separate the classes by age was a complete failure. No reasonable age grouping had enough members to form a class and half of the adult ladies had to be Sunday school teachers to cover all of the small classes. Often an entire class would be absent on a given Sunday. This was an attempt to copy the organization of the big church in Superior where every grade had its own class and lots of students for each. Their large congregation allows selection of teachers and backup teachers and teacher assistants and substitute teachers and rotation of teachers when burnout happens.

When the classes were divided into two classes: 1) Adults and 2) Kids, the preacher was fine teaching the adult class, but boys showing off for girls, tormenting them with spitballs and hair tugs and funny faces made the Kids class unmanageable. One deacon's wife threatened to stop attending church because the disorder made her nervous. Needless to say, separating the boys and girls went a long way toward restoring order in the Sunday school.

Mrs. Knutson turned the Boys class over to Mrs. Iverson for a while when her pregnancy caused morning sickness and swelling of the feet when standing in front of the class. She doesn't sit while teaching that class because a quick intervention is often needed when one of the boys forgets he is in Sunday school instead of on the playground. We are sternly warned by the preacher that he will take harsh disciplinary measures if anyone gives Mrs. Iverson any trouble. The real threat is that our parents will find out about misbehavior and we will face disciplinary action when we get home.

No one forgets the time Johnny Erikson started fussing with his sister during the preaching service. His dad grabs him by the left ear and marches him right down the center aisle with his head sidewise, hopping along to prevent his ear from being pulled out by the roots. When they get outside, George Erikson lets go of Johnny's ear to take the belt out of his trousers. Johnny knows what is to follow and takes off running toward the back of the church with his dad in hot pursuit. The church windows are all open.

Everyone's attention is on the drama unfolding as the participant's race by the open church windows. The preaching stops as the preacher finds himself monitoring the progress of Johnny's escape attempt. On the second lap, Johnny realizes everyone is watching.

He hollers out "Pray for me!"

Just then, George Erikson's trousers slip to his ankles due to an absence of belt suspension. George trips and rolls on the church lawn. The entire congregation moves to the windows on that side of the church to watch George hurriedly pull up his trousers and reinsert the belt.

Johnny and his dad re-enter the church and sit together in the back pew. Everyone turns their attention back to the front of the church to hear the rest of the Sermon. The preacher's notes were knocked to the floor during the distraction. He spends a couple of minutes trying to put them back in order. He is unable to remember where he was when the distraction began. He takes his glasses off and cleans them. He tries to figure out how to proceed. He takes a drink of water as everyone waits expectantly. He leans on the pulpit and mops his brow. It gets hot in the little church in July even with the windows open. He finally admits that his sermon can not be salvaged. He will rework the sermon for next Sunday.

The preacher opines that God answers prayer. That point is proven when the congregation witnessed an immediate answer to Johnny's prayer. He says, "All things work together for good to them that love the Lord." He says, "George, go easy on Johnny since he was directed of the Holy Spirit to bring this lesson to the church." We are dismissed early from church. This is one of the few sermons remembered after its delivery. I don't recall what the preacher was getting at prior to Johnny's demonstration of the power of prayer, even though he repeated that sermon again the next Sunday.

We all know that discipline at home is the real impediment to misbehavior. Mrs. Iverson's advanced age and poor hearing is not to be challenged. Mrs. Iverson decides to prove her teaching skills with a presentation of real Bible knowledge to the congregation by the Boy's class. She copies the Beatitudes from Mathew 5.

In case you forgot them they are:

1. Blessed are the poor in spirit, for theirs is the kingdom of heaven.
2. Blessed are those who mourn, for they will be comforted.
3. Blessed are the meek, for they will inherit the earth.
4. Blessed are those who hunger and thirst for righteousness, for they will be filled.
5. Blessed are the merciful, for they will be shown mercy.
6. Blessed are the pure in heart, for they will see God.
7. Blessed are the peacemakers, for they will be called the children of God.
8. Blessed are those who are persecuted because of righteousness, for theirs is the kingdom of heaven.
9. Blessed are you when people insult you, persecute you and falsely say all kinds of evil against you because of me, because great is your reward in heaven.

Each member of the Boy's class is assigned one beatitude. Since there are 10 regular members, she adds the next item from Matthew 5: You are the salt of the earth. Stay salty!" which will precede the presentation of the beatitudes.

Mrs. Iverson assigns each beatitude according to her assessment of the student's aptitude. Joey is a slow learner so he is given his choice. He chooses number seven because he likes the joke Sam made: "Blessed are the Peacemakers, for they tamed the West." Sam also said: "Blessed are the meek, for they are easy to intimidate." Mrs. Iverson threatens to report Sam's impudence to the preacher and the jokes stop.

I ask to do number nine since it is the last and longest beatitude. I like to talk as you may have noticed. Sam is assigned number three because he needs to remember the real idea instead of his joke.

We each take our beatitude home for memorization. Next Sunday we will practice our parts for presentation as opening to the preaching service. We arrive Sunday morning and find each class member well prepared for the demonstration of Bible knowledge imparted by the skillful tutelage of Mrs. Iverson. She has us stand in the order of our particular beatitude with John first presenting his Salt of the earth quote. Sunday school lasts an hour and we have gone over our parts several times. Mrs. Iverson tells Sam he has to read his beatitude because he twice said "for they are easy to intimidate" during practice instead of finishing with "for they will inherit the earth". Sam is humbled because he has to read his beatitude while everyone else is trusted to recite theirs from memory.

The bell rings and class is over.

We are ready!

The preacher announces that the Boy's class has a special presentation and calls us to the platform. He didn't coordinate with Mrs. Iverson so he lines us up on the platform out of order. We are a sharp group, so the salt of the earth recitation and beatitudes 1 and 2 are presented perfectly. Joey is standing next to Tony who recites beatitude number two. He belts out "Blessed are the peacemakers, for they will be called the children of God". It was Sam's turn!

Sam glares at Tony and hits him in the shoulder so hard it almost knocks him over. Mrs. Iverson, standing to one side places both hands to the side of her face and sits down in the platform chair. I must restore order and dignity, a feat which I would ordinarily achieve with the mere raising of the great notched sword. I am not allowed to bring my weapon to church. I have no option except to tackle Sam. Joey jumps on top of both of us with fists flailing. The entire Boys class is piled on the stage each hitting, pulling and shoving in an attempt to restore order. Parents surge forward, each pulling his particular child from the fray. Merlin grabs my belt and hauls me unceremoniously to the pew beside him where he leans over to whisper, "You done good. I just grabbed you to save you from King Arthur's wrath."

Mrs. Iverson resigns from teaching the Boys class.

BLACKIE

A group of pine and birch and poplar scrub trees is nestled in behind the chicken coop providing afternoon shade to the fenced-in chicken yard and a home for thieving crows that are all too happy to share cracked corn kernels with the chickens instead of hunting their own food. One brazen crow family built a nest right there in a poplar tree so they wouldn't have to work so hard to feed their young.

Crows are smart, wary birds. It is hard to get close enough to fling a rock at them to chase them away from the chicken feed. We often tried unsuccessfully. Even if you hide and wait for them, they figure it out and won't come until you leave. Crows are just tolerated by the farmers since they eat crops, but they aren't so bad that any real effort is expended to get rid of them.

Sir Lancelot and the armor bearers head to the chicken yard at a dead run when a huge ruckus erupts among the chickens. We figure a weasel or raccoon or fox or large snake or something is after the chickens. I lead the charge with sword held high, expecting some sort of memorable adventure is about to unfold.

I tell the armor bearers, "Stay back if it turns out to be a dragon or lion as only I am equipped to handle such beasts."

We yell at the top of our lungs so a cowardly beast will have a chance to flee without endangering either him or us. What's this? Two crows are dive bombing the chickens.

They normally just strut in among the chickens and share food like they are little black chickens. Are the crows going to try to eat chickens? They eat most anything, but I never heard of a crow eating a chicken. We do have hawks that will attempt to haul off a chicken, but even a big hawk is at his limit trying to fly off with a full grown chicken in his claws. We had one hawk land in the chicken yard two weeks ago and attempt to fly off with a chicken he had killed. He was unable to get enough flying speed to clear the chicken wire fence. King Arthur dispatched that hawk to the Promised Land with a mighty blow from a dead tree limb. It would have been another notch on my sword if I had gotten there in time.

The crime scene became clearer as we neared the racket of screaming crows and squawking chickens and screeching guinea hens. A fledgling baby crow had fallen from the nest and the chickens were trying to attack the baby bird. The crow's parents were driving the chickens off as they tried to peck at the baby bird. Most of the chickens had no idea what was going on. They were just squawking because the others were squawking. The crow's parents didn't fly off as we approached. They saw us as more threats to their offspring and flew right at us as well.

We normally see crows as a nuisance and attempt to drive them off, but we can't allow the chickens to harass the baby bird. We chase the chickens away from the frightened squawking baby bird while holding our arms over our heads to ward off the baby crow's parents who are flying at us so close that they actually hit us with their wings several times.

I bend down and pick up the frightened baby bird that is shivering in fear and inspect him for injury. It doesn't seem like he is hurt at all. The baby crow's parents fly to the top of the pine tree and watch. I realize that the nest is far too high for me to replace the fledgling crow in its nest. I decide to place the little fellow up as high as I can for safety and his parents might then care for him there.

The armor bearers head for the woodshed to get an old wooden box. We wedge the box into a crotch in the poplar tree holding the crow's nest. We pull up some dry grass and put it in the bottom of the box so the little fellow will be comfortable. We get an old sardine tin to put some water in. This should surely be a more comfortable home for the crow family than the pile of sticks they have been calling home.

This is a lot of fun and we feel noble about our care for the helpless baby crow. Still it is a little disappointing on the adventure scale when you consider that our biggest threat was being whacked by crow feathers. One of the armor bearers thought there should be a notch carved on the sword since the crows could have pecked our eyes out. We decide to discuss the merits of this adventure with Merlin before ruling it out as a full fledged adventure.

One would expect that the episode is over and done. We walk to the house to discuss the matter and retrieve the rest of the eggs we collected earlier. Guinevere agreed that we did the right thing to save the baby crow even if his parents were thieves. We named the little fellow Blackie so we could discuss the proceedings in a more coherent way. You can't properly refer to a thing unless you first name it. We checked the box from a distance many times that day, not getting too near it so as to scare Blackie Pop and Blackie Mom away. Blackie seemed to just sit still in the box shivering a bit and not inspecting his home or taking any water. Blackie Pop and Mom never went near the box. In fact, they never returned to their old nest.

We kept our distance from the box most of the next day so as not to scare mom and pop away, but they never returned. Blackie is abandoned by his own parents. It isn't our fault. We tried to help but they refuse to accept our philanthropy. We decide it is our duty to care for the orphaned Blackie.

We try to put water in his mouth with a spoon. Guinevere becomes interested in the project and brings out an old medicine dropper with which we nearly drown poor Blackie. None of us have any idea how to care for a baby crow that doesn't even have most of its feathers. We ask Merlin what crows eat.

He says "They will eat anything."

We told him "This crow won't eat cracked corn, Cheerios, Wheaties, Rice Crispi's, bits of cheese or bits of bologna.

Merlin says "He may be too frightened to eat and will probably die. "

We decide that Blackie is now our responsibility and we have to find a way to feed him. One of the armor bearers finds a white grub growing in the stalk of a weed in the pasture. We know about those grubs because

Merlin sometimes collects them for fishing bait. Blackie gulps the grub down. Persistence pays off.

Six boys can collect a lot of grubs when there are forty acres of pasture and the cows won't eat the weeds that the grubs inhabit. Within a few days Blackie comes to the edge of the box whenever we approach. He squawks and open his mouth for dinner. He doesn't like us squirting the water in his mouth with the medicine dropper. He shakes his head side to side to fling the water away. We think he needs a bit of water and give him a bit every time we feed him. Within a week and a half, Blackie has a lot of feathers and stands on the edge of the box and flaps his wings. I think he is the fattest baby crow in the land.

We are disappointed to find the box empty one morning. Something has happened to Blackie. We search the area, thinking he might have fallen to the ground and scooted off to hide somewhere. The armor bearers who are out collecting grubs come to the box where I give them the sad news. Blackie is gone.

I nearly fall to my knees when Blackie swoops down and lands on my shoulder. He was sitting high up in the poplar tree watching the whole thing. He leans his head back for his grubs. After we all pet him and welcome him back, we set him back in his box. He immediately flies to a branch a few feet higher and works his way far up into the tree. We all grab hands and dance in a ring around the rosy and all fall down laughing in celebration. Blackie discovers ways to get food all by himself, but immediately lands on the shoulder of anyone carrying a handful of grubs.

He doesn't stay in the box in the poplar tree any longer. We don't know where he spends most of his time. We never see him flying with the other crows around the farm. Blackie can spot anyone with a handful of grubs and land on them, gorging himself until the grubs are gone. He now eats nearly anything offered from bits of table scraps to bread and sometimes whatever you have in your hand and plan to eat yourself. Blackie sits on the drainpipe over the kitchen door waiting for someone to come out and throw something in the air for him to eat in the morning.

Blackie becomes a bigger nuisance every day. Instead of flying away when people are around, he flies to them and lands on their head or their shoulder. Blackie will hang around anyone working outside. When Guinevere hangs clothes on the clothesline, Blackie sits on the clothes poles and watches. He lands on blankets and big things that are easy to grasp with his claws. Then he begins pulling the clothespins out, dropping the drying clothes on the ground. Guinevere tries to shoo him away.

Blackie thinks it is a great game and pulls out clothespins just to get her to play with him. The pastor comes over for dinner and counseling one evening and doesn't see Blackie until he lands on his head, knocking his toupee sideways. Blackie is startled by the loose hair and flaps his wings in mighty beats to regain his balance and fly off, taking the toupee with him. It is dropped on top of the lilac bush. Merlin laughs so hard he falls off the porch and nearly hurts himself. The pastor threatens not to stay for chicken dinner because Merlin said "The toupee looks better on the lilac bush than on your head."

Guinevere smooths everything over when she announces that dinner is on the table. The pastor forgets his threat of leaving without completing his pastoral duties.

The pastor says "Blackie reminds me of the devil with his black coat and evil eyes.

Guinevere said "Blackie is a greater nuisance around the house than the devil himself.

King Arthur is double teamed by Guinevere and the pastor. Blackie's supporters are powerless. No one can deny that Blackie is a nuisance who's only redeeming quality is entertainment.

King Arthur banishes Blackie from the Kingdom. We all pile in the car including Blackie who is lured in with a handful of grubs. We drive to Superior to get sugar and salt and flower and some fence repair materials. We let Blackie out of the car down by the giant grain elevators where a lot of crows hang out. Blackie flies to the top of a bridge where he is sitting as we drive away.

We never see Blackie again. We hear stories about a crow pulling clothes pins out of drying laundry and suspect Blackie is out there being a nuisance to someone else.

BOUNTY HUNTER

A great warrior like Sir Lancelot fights dragons and lions and bears and wolves simply because it is his responsibility to protect the Kingdom of Johnson. In general, the larger the predator, the greater is the threat. Smaller predators can also cause great harm, so they must also be guarded against. A Knight's reputation for bravery and heroism is enhanced more in battle against large dangerous foes than in fighting small vermin and insects. The small foes are not to be underestimated though. A swarm of grasshoppers can wipe out a field of wheat, a little hornet can kill a heavily armed knight and a rat can multiply into a herd of rats capable of eating a whole crib full of corn if left unopposed.

Foxes are clever creatures capable of raiding chicken houses where they eat chickens and eggs. The County Agricultural Agent has received many complaints of foxes raiding chicken houses in Douglas County. It seems that fewer trappers are trapping fox for their beautiful fur since the advent of commercial mink and chinchilla farms. A mink coat sounds more luxurious than a fox fur coat. Whatever may be the cause, the fox population is exploding. The County Agent placed a bounty of twenty five cents on each fox in an attempt to remain electable next election. Since he has run unopposed for the past twenty years, his job is under no real threat. Politicians like to believe they are elected by an informed electorate who elect them due to their record of achievement. It will provide fodder for a Fourth of July political speech if he can say he solved the fox problem during his term of office.

King Arthur and Merlin talk about setting a few fox traps around the farm buildings. Twenty five cents bounty money isn't a huge incentive, but the fur is worth an additional dollar and a quarter making it worth the trouble to trap and skin a few thieving foxes. Serious fox hunters go out in the woods with dogs to route the foxes from their dens where they can be dispatched by a well placed shot from a 22 caliber rifle. We don't have any fox hounds.

Fox hunting is mostly a sport for young men who need to have excitement at night and then can get up in the morning and do a days work without proper sleep. King Arthur and Merlin decide against trapping the foxes as they might inadvertently trap one of the cats or some other creature. I am impressed at the way they can let the opportunity for big money pass them by. It takes twelve dozen eggs to bring in a dollar and a half.

I dream of catching a fox with a chicken in its mouth. I will slay the fox with my trusty sword and share all the money with the armor bearers who will admire my skill and generosity. The County Agent may mention my contribution to the county in his Fourth of July speech. I revel in the imagined fame.

I advise the armor bearers "Be on the alert for signs of fox around the hen house." We suspect a fox may actually be raiding the hen house as feathers near the hen house and broken eggs suggest a thieving fox is about.

Merlin says "I will get that fox which is getting so bold as to come right onto the farm at night."

He loads the double barreled Winchester shotgun with buckshot and places it on pegs over the porch door. It will be handy if a fox comes around.

I am dreaming of fame and fortune when I hear a ruckus in the hen house. I leap from bed and rush to inform Merlin. He leaps from bed in his nightshirt and heads down the stairs three steps at a time. I scurry after him to share the excitement. Merlin grabs a flashlight off the shelf and tucks the shotgun under his arm. The racket coming from the hen house seems to increase as we jump off the porch and run toward the hen house.

I didn't have time to grab the great notched sword in my haste. I regret being unarmed, but Merlin and the shotgun should be adequate. I think that brazen fox must be sitting in the hen house having a feast instead of a more likely hit and run raid. We will have good reason to dispatch of this marauder if we find him in the act of dining on one of Guinevere's laying hens.

Merlin jerks the hen house door open holding the flashlight and shotgun at the ready as he plays the light beam across the fluttering, squawking flock of chickens. There it is! Hiding in the farthest corner of the hen house is a fox holding an unfortunate chicken by the neck. Merlin raises the shotgun and says "Hold the light." This is almost as good as me pressing the attack.

I grab the light and start to point it at the fox so Merlin can get a good aim. I hear a noise beside me and quickly swing the light toward the noise as my heart leaps into my throat. Is there new danger lurking in the darkness? Is there a whole pack of foxes here to protect their brother fox? If only I had grabbed my sword on the way out!

I shine the light into the eyes of a great beast running at us.

Merlin shouts "shine the light on him!" as he attempts to see the fox in the dark hen house.

My voice fails me as I attempt to warn Merlin of the new danger. As my knees are about to give way, I realize that the charging beast is Old Blue, the Anderson's fox hunting blue tick hound. I swing the light back into the hen house as old blue arrives on the scene to assist in the fox hunt.

I didn't realize that Merlin was unaware of our hunting assistant's arrival. Merlin and I are concentrating on getting the fox located when Old Blue does his dog greeting. He pushes his cold nose up under Merlin's night shirt to smell his behind. Merlin is so surprised at the cold wet nose on his bottom in friendly dog greeting that both barrels of the shotgun are discharged with no particular target.

The Kick of the unplanned shotgun discharge knocks Merlin off balance and he trips over me and Old Blue. We are flat on our backs in the dark with the shotgun inside the hen house. The fox runs right over the pile of people and dog in panicked escape mode. Old Blue recovers first and leaps away in pursuit of the fox, baying in his deep dog voice to let the Anderson boys know he has flushed a fox.

I hunt around in the dark for the flashlight that went out when I dropped it.

Merlin, still not aware that Old Blue had stopped in to help us, asks in a surprised tone "What was that?"

Merlin sits on the ground and laughs so hard that tears come to his eyes when I tell him that Old Blue was trying to help us get the fox.

Merlin says, " Old Blue should learn that meeting people has a different protocol than meeting a new dog.

The squawking in the hen house is louder now than it was when we first arrived. I find the flashlight and switch it back on as Old Blue's baying fades into the distance. We survey the damage. There is a hole in the back wall of the hen house. Five hens are dead and a sixth one is injured and has to be butchered as well.

Merlin and I discuss the incident at length on our way back to the house. Merlin is carrying the shotgun and four chickens and I am carrying the flashlight and two chickens. The chicken heads are chopped off to let the blood drain out for butchering. Merlin places the shotgun back on its pegs over the kitchen door.

He says "we sure scared that fox! I'll bet he doesn't raid our hen house again for a while!"

The big canning kettle is on the stove with water starting to boil so we can scald the chicken feathers in preparation for plucking when Guinevere asks "What are you doing?" from the top of the stairs.

Merlin answers "We decided we would like a chicken dinner tomorrow and are butchering some chickens for that event."

Puzzled, Guinevere comes down to investigate and asks "Why did you decide to butcher six chickens when two would have been plenty?"

Merlin explains "We might want to invite the preacher and the Andersons over since their dog helped us butcher the chickens. The preacher is always hungry."

Guinevere shakes her head and goes back to bed muttering something about living in a house full of crazy people.

Merlin and I pluck the chickens and cut them up into frying sized pieces. We take the feathers and entrails out to the manure pile for disposal. We still haven't decided if we are going to share the story of the chicken massacre with the rest of the family as we place the chickens in the ice box.

I ask Merlin "How are you going to explain what happened."

He says "It wouldn't be fair to blame it on Old Blue as his intentions were good. Maybe this night's events should remain a mystery."

THE RAT KILLING

Sir Lancelot and the armor bearers are always on the alert for threats to the Kingdom of Johnson. This morning we are full of breakfast and energy and enthusiasm. The sun is shining and we have collected all the eggs in known nests. We have the wire basket nearly full of eggs. We are now spread out all around the farm buildings looking in corners and behind old boards for new nesting sites. All of the silage has been thrown out of the silo to feed the cows through the winter. Silage is used as a food supplement to oats and ground corn and hay through the long cold Wisconsin winters.

The silo soars thirty feet above the ground right next to the barn. It has a tin dome on top to keep out rain which gives it a regal appearance. We consider the silo to be a defense tower at the corner of the castle. The silo and the windmill are the tallest structures on the farm. The height of the silo and windmill are two sources of pride on every farm. The Olsen's have two silos on their farm. The second silo is forty five feet high. Farmers with shorter silos can be heard to criticize Mr. Olsen's tall silo. They say it is hard to blow silage so high to fill the silo. They say it takes too long to feed the silage all the way to the bottom. They say the extra height costs too much because it requires extra strong footers to hold all the weight. Some just consider it extravagant. The tall silo dwarfs the shorter silo causing asymmetry which is less attractive than buildings complementing each other in their proportions and placement. In other words, everyone envies Mr. Olsen's silo and has a good excuse for not owning such a grand structure of his own.

We are proud of our more modest silo. It has a ladder up the outside. The outside ladder is only used to assemble the sections of pipe which carry silage from the chopper/blower into an opening in the tin dome on top. Silage is chopped and blown up the pipe by a huge rotary chopper fan. The fan is driven by a belt attached to a pulley on the old 10-20 McCormick/Deering tractor. The old tractor is a frightful machine. It has huge steel wheels on the rear with cleats welded on for traction. It can run on kerosene or gasoline. It has three tanks over the massive engine. The small tank holds gasoline which is used to start the engine. The largest tank holds kerosene which is less expensive than gasoline and provides more power. The third tank holds water which is fed in with the kerosene when the engine is really pulling hard and the exhaust manifold is glowing bright red. Merlin says the steam from the water ads power and keeps the engine running at the proper temperature. A compression release lever reduces the compression for starting the engine.

It takes a skilled operator just to start the beast. The kerosene and water must be shut off which is always done at the time the engine is stopped. The gasoline line is turned on and a primer pump is pumped to get gasoline to the cylinders. The magneto switch is turned on and the compression release lever is forward. Merlin emphasizes that the most important preparation is to see that the shift lever is in neutral. The engine starts on the first pull on the crank and the tractor will start moving if it is in gear. This has happened to more than one careless farmer. The Jensen boy was seriously injured when he started their tractor and it hit the side of the machine shed, knocking the entire shed apart and dropping rafters onto the hapless boy who was trying to get the beast stopped.

One pull of the crank usually starts the engine. It chugs to life with little power and lots of noise and smoke. Now it is time to advance the spark, increase throttle setting and pull the compression lever back to let the engine warm up. The throttle is then advanced creating a roar. The high energy gasoline quickly heats the engine and kerosene is slowly introduced as gasoline flow is reduced and stopped. Black smoke pours out of the exhaust stack until the engine heats to full operating temperature. When the exhaust manifold is cherry red and the exhaust is white, water is gradually trickled into the mixture increasing the density of the white exhaust and reducing the brightness of the glowing red exhaust manifold. The tractor is now ready to work. The belt is looped over the belt pulley and the tractor is backed up to tighten the belt. The brake lever is locked. When the belt pulley gear is engaged, the silage chopper/blower begins to howl. Corn stalks are fed to the blower and they are chopped into bits and blown up the pipe to fill the silo.

Silo filling is an exciting time. Several farmers get together to fill each others silos. One set of silo filling equipment serves several farms. One man cuts the corn in the field with a tractor drawn corn binder that cuts the stalks and ties them into small bundles dropping them on the ground. A second man pulls a wagon through the field while two others load the bundles of corn stalks onto the wagon. They pull the wagon up to the corn chopper/blower where they exchange the loaded wagon for an empty one and head back for another load. Another farmer feeds the corn bundles into the chopper, filling the silo. It may take three days to fill a silo. The silo filling crew then moves on to the next farm in a cooperative sharing of equipment and labor. The women gather at the farm house where great feasts are prepared for the evening and sandwiches and water and Kool Aid are supplied through the day for the work crew. The ladies exchange a lot of information during these cooperative events.

Just looking at a silo is exciting to one who has observed a silo filling. The silo also has an enclosed ladder which opens into the barn. This ladder is used to climb to the tope of the pile of silage and is the chute where each day's portion of silage feed is thrown for distribution to hungry livestock. Boards are removed from the inside ladder as the silage height is reduced with usage, allowing silage to be thrown into the chute easily. Now that the silo has been emptied, the bottom of the silo six feet below ground level is exposed.

An armor bearer hears a noise and looks into the empty silo to see if a hen has selected the empty silo as a nest site. To his surprise, a large rat is sitting in the bottom of the empty silo. It seems unable to climb out. We gather to stare at the trapped creature. We know that rats eat our grain and create stinky nests in the corn bins. I have yet to hear of one redeeming feature attached to these rascals. Raccoons create a lot of the same problems, but they are pretty and can be trapped for their hides and even eaten. They can be entertaining creatures. Rats are ugly and spread disease and damage food stores.

This rat has to go!

We have several cats that wander around the farm to control the rat and mouse population. It's time for the cats to earn their keep. We play with the kittens and feed them when they are little, but the cats become pretty independent after that. We don't feed them on any regular schedule to encourage their hunting activity. Tom is the king of the cats. He is a giant orange tom cat. Tom is a scarred veteran of many battles with rival male cats and other creatures foolish enough to tackle a tiger cat. He might be more tiger than cat. Tom was hanging around the barn this morning after milking time because Merlin had set out a dish of milk. I saw Tom sleeping on some hay in the manger while looking for new nests earlier. We post an armor bearer at the silo with a stick to be sure the rat doesn't escape.

We go hunting for Tom. We find him stretched out in the sun next to the wood shed. He allows us to carry him to the silo where the trapped rat is scurrying around looking for an escape. Tom doesn't view the rat as food since he filled up on milk this morning. Guinevere is right. Feeding the cats too much will discourage them from doing their intended duty of protecting the Kingdom from vermin.

Tom is leaning forward to look at the rat, so we encourage him with a shove. He does the cat thing well, landing on his feet even after such an unceremonious launch. The rat hunches down, eyeing Tom, daring him to get nearer. Tom crouches down staring at the rat. We shout encouragement to the gladiators. We feel no guilt over our bloodthirsty excitement. We are merely bringing justice to a criminal.

Tom leaps at the rat which squeals and rolls underneath Tom's attack. Surprisingly the rat doesn't flee in terror, but attacks Tom and the action becomes so fast and furious that it is hard to follow. Tom is snarling and leaping from the fray and then turning to leap back in. The cornered rat never turns his back on Tom to flee. He even presses the attack. Tom has had enough of the fracas.

He leaps out of the silo bottom with a torn ear and races out of the barn. We are so astonished at Tom's behavior that we forget to guard against the rat's escape. The rat scurries from the confines of the silo. He cannot run very fast. We pursue him with the stick and my great notched sword harassing his escape.

The rat turns and sits up threatening to attack us and we back off. He then turns to run and we resume the harassment, striking at him with the stick and my sword. He again turns and sits up threatening to attack us and we nearly knock each other over backing away. The process repeats itself a dozen times all the way across the barnyard, disturbing the cows as we pass. The rat scurries under the fence toward the orchard next to the lane where we have a few choke cherry trees and crab apple trees.

The choke cherries are tiny and mostly seed. They are messy eating as they turn your hands dark purple from their juice. We gather whole wash tubs full of choke cherries in the fall. Guinevere then cooks them to soften them. She puts the cherry mash into a white cloth bag and twists the bag, squeezing out the juice. Sure Gel and sugar are added and the cherry jelly is canned. We get some on our breakfast toast at times, but most of it is given to friends and neighbors as a gift at appropriate times. Mom's choke cherry jelly has won first prize at the fair two times.

The crab apples are tiny and sour. We start eating them as soon as they are big enough even though the green apples are sour and will give you a stomach ache if more than a couple are eaten. We pick bushels of the tiny apples as soon as they are partly red. They fall on the ground shortly after that and are unusable. The apples are cored and cooked with all the bad spots cut out. They become apple butter, apple jelly, and apple juice. Guinevere says they are not the right kind of apples for apple pie so the apples for pie are traded from the Olsens in exchange for some of our eggs.

Guinevere says "The choke cherries and crab apples are more work than they are worth." The blossoms are so pretty and fragrant in the spring she won't allow them to be cut down.

We see the rat heading for an apple tree as we race to the gate in order to continue our pursuit. We race to the tree where the rat was last sighted. He is nowhere to be seen. We would have seen him if he continued through the orchard. The grass is short with a lot of bare ground. We return to the last place he was sighted at the base of an old crab apple tree.

Aha! We have him! The old tree is hollow with an opening at its base. The rat must have crawled into the tree to hide. We pick up some fallen tree limbs and beat on the trunk of the tree to scare him out.

Nothing!

We sit on the ground around the tree discussing ways to get him out so we can administer proper justice for his error of being a rat. Two armor bearers leave to search for Tom who has a score to settle with this particular rat. They return with Tom, but he exhibits no interest in the hollow tree and is too big to get into the hole at its base.

We decide that we must smoke the rat out.

I know that Guinevere is a bit timid and will kill the project if we reveal our plans. The rat may escape if we try to guard his hideout until Merlin and King Arthur are free to assist us. It is my job to surreptitiously obtain matches so we can smoke the vermin out of his lair. The rest of us will collect materials for a fire and guard the tree. Mine is the hardest job as I must obtain a match without raising suspicion about its use.

The carefully planned subterfuge is under way. I take my most trusted armor bearer to the pasture where he steps into a fresh cow pie, getting a bit on his stocking as well. We then walk to the house to show Guinevere his soiled foot. As predicted, she orders him into the bathroom where his shoe is wiped clean and the stocking is rinsed out. She then goes to the sock drawer upstairs to get clean socks. As soon as she starts up the stairs, I pull a chair to the stove and climb on it to get two matches out of the matchbox stored on the shelf behind the stove. I pull a few sheets of toilet paper off the roll after returning the chair to the table. I then sit on the chair and wait for my companion to get his clean socks. The toilet paper should make it easier to start the fire, but it is nearly our undoing.

175

Guinevere asks why I have toilet paper in my pocket. I didn't push it in far enough. I stammer a bit until my heart quits racing. I say that it is always good to have a handkerchief. Guinevere is satisfied with my answer since she is always trying to get me to be more careful with hygiene. We head for the orchard at a run. A pile of sticks and dry grass is waiting. We have a long discussion about the ethics of obtaining the matches by trickery. Might we have merely asked for them? I convince everyone that our purpose is honorable and no other means of carrying out our plan to rid the farm of the rat would work. Machiavelli teaches us that the ends justify the means. We are on solid ethical ground with our good intentions!

I take out the toilet paper and pile small sticks and dried grass over it. A match is struck on a dry rock and it bursts into flame. A light breeze extinguishes the match as I move it toward the prepared tinder pile. I have only one more match. I wish I had grabbed several more. No one counts matches in the match box. Hind sight is so much better than foresight. The armor bearers sit shoulder to shoulder blocking the wind as I light our last match right next to the tinder pile. The carefully prepared incendiary material ignites immediately. The dry material is nearly burned up, starving the fire of fuel, before we add more material to the flames. We carefully push the burning pile of sticks into the hole in the base of the old tree.

Now we can add flammable material to the fire at will. We accumulate enough sticks to keep a house warm for a week. It is tempting to keep adding to the fire, but it might get away from us if we make it any bigger. I stand

176

by with my sword raised to execute the rat when he appears.

No rat appears.

We now begin to pile green leaves and grass on the fire increasing the smoke density. The rat will have to come out if the smoke gets so thick he can't breathe. Two armor bearers go to the milk house for pails of water to put the fire out when we are done. We finally have to put the fire out when we are called for dinner. The rat hasn't appeared.

We realize that he might not be in the hollow tree after all. The water is used to completely extinguish the burning sticks and the rest is thrown into the hole at the bottom or the tree. We have to go in for lunch since this is the second time we are called. It is really disappointing to fail in such a well planned venture.

After lunch and brief naps, the armor bearers are imprisoned in the sand box prison and I am sitting outside the fence discussing what went wrong with our rat killing plans. We decide the rat must have kept on going past the tree. As we are discussing that possibility we notice a wisp of smoke coming from the orchard.

I run to the orchard to check on the fire. There is no fire around the tree or opening to its hollow center. Smoke is coming from branches on the tree. We set the dead interior of the tree on fire. There are no open flames. The rotten dead center of the tree is smoldering. I move all of the flammable material away from the tree. I carry bucket after bucket of water from the milk house and throw it on the tree and into the hole at its base, but nothing changes. The tree continues to smolder.

I rush to the orchard first thing in the morning. All the leaves have fallen off the branches of the apple tree. Tiny crab apples, the size of a ping pong ball, hang from the branches of the smoking tree in perfusion no longer hidden amongst leaves. Should I confess to my crime of apple tree killer? Maybe the fire will go out and the tree will be ok. I'll wait a while since there is no urgency in turning myself in.

It has been two days since we set the tree on fire and the apples are now falling off. What next? Tendrils of smoke continue to emanate from branches of the dying tree. I don't think the tree will produce any apples this year. I broach the topic at lunch,

I tell Guinevere "One of the crab apple trees doesn't seem to be growing any apples this year."

I am relieved to hear her respond "I enjoy the blossoms more than the apples anyway. Beside, it is too early to predict the size of the apple crop."

I continue to check the tree every morning. My heart sinks as the wisps of smoke continue to waft into the air around the dead apple tree. Now great pieces of bark are falling from the branches near the trunk. The tree is dead.

The guilt is too heavy to bear any longer.

I call for a meeting of the Round Table.

Merlin asks "What adventure occasions this meeting?"

I explain "I killed a tree."

178

Merlin says "Killing a tree isn't going to earn you a notch on your sword unless it is a really evil tree."

I confess "It was a good and innocent tree."

Merlin asks "Why did you kill the tree?"

I explain "Killing the tree was an accident. I was trying to kill a rat."

Merlin nearly falls off the porch in a fit of laughter. He points at me and says "You mistook a tree for a rat?" He says "I will wait for the rest of the story at the Round Table tonight."

I feel a bit better since it seems Merlin and Guinevere aren't too upset about the tree.

WALTER

Sir Lancelot, the armor bearers, King Arthur, Guinevere and Merlin all crowd into the big Buick. The trunk is full of canned vegetables and fruits and even a couple jars of fish balls. We are off on a charitable mission. Walter Noland is to be recipient of these fruits of our labor.

Merlin asks King Arthur to stop next to the smoke house so he can put a smoked ham on top of the boxes of other food. Merlin is the only one in the car who even likes Walter. The other adults shake their heads and wonder how Walter can live like he does whenever his name comes up.

Walter isn't commonly a topic of discussion in the Kingdom of Johnson. I'm told his name comes up often at the Missionary Sewing Circle where the church ladies tear worn bed sheets into long strips and roll them up to be used as bandages by the missionaries. They gather worn clothing and repair it with patches to be worn by children in far off lands. They discuss how to win sinners to a right way of living near and far. I suspect it is in this context that Walter's name comes up. A long time ago Guinevere mentioned Walter at our breakfast table when the topic of drunkenness was brought up.

She said "No one is worthless! Even Walter can be used as a bad example."

Merlin was furious at that comment. He said "I respect Walter more than any of the ladies in the sewing circle who know nothing of heroism, adversity and tragedy."

Wow!

That is the only time I've ever seen Merlin angry. He gets along with everyone and especially everyone in our home.

Mom apologized for her careless criticism and the tempest was over.

Now we are in route to Walter's dilapidated old farmhouse with gifts of food. This isn't especially remarkable. Nearly every farm family in the area brings food and clothes to Walter from time to time. He is the perfect target of charity.

Walter lives in the same house his father built when he immigrated to northern Wisconsin in 1885. The house originally had two rooms. A lean-to was attached to one side for goats, sheep, pigs and chickens. I don't think the Nolands ever had cattle or horses. A third room was added when little Walter came along. Walter's dad worked long hours at the saw mill. He purchased more land every time he was able. They didn't work the land except for a huge garden maintained by Walter's mom. Walter and his father both went off to France to fight the Great War. Walter's father died in a German prison camp. Walter lost a leg to an artillery shell exploding in the trench near him. The rest of his company of eight was killed by the explosion as it set off their own ammunition store.

Merlin described Walter's history and expressed admiration that a man could survive such tragedy.

Merlin said "Walter has wished for death ever since his return from the war. His mom grieved Walter's loss and her husband's death to the point that she stopped eating and died two years later herself. Walter was engaged to Ruth Benet when he went off to war. He returned to find Ruth pregnant and married to Al Rosen. From then on, Walter stayed drunk if he was able to get liquor. Walter receives a meager veteran's pension which he spends entirely on liquor. From time to time he will sell a parcel of land. He now lives in the old farm house on five acres with goats, sheep, and chickens in the lean-to. He allows the animals into the house when it is cold or wet outside. He has probably not had a bath since dating Ruth at 17 years of age. Did I mention that Walter smells badly?

He does!

We round a corner on the dirt road that leads to Walter's shack and see Walter driving toward us in his old Model T touring car. His is the only Model T still in use around these parts. The car was once black, but dirt and rust have long since turned it to a muddy reddish brown color. The seats long ago rotted and have been removed. Walter drives sitting on a box covered with old rags. Walter often has a couple of his animals in the car with him. He says they all like to ride in the car and they are good company. King Arthur stops the Buick and waves Walter over.

Walter says "I am on the way to Superior to pick up some supplies.

King Arthur says "we are on our way to bring you some winter food supplies."

Walter says "My trip to Superior is urgent."

He is shaking a lot and is clearly in need of a drink.

Merlin says "I have a special gift for you and would like to share it with you right now."

Walter shuts down the Model T and climbs over the door. Merlin walks around the Buick to shake Walter's hand and then pull him into a great bear hug. King Arthur smiles and gets out when Merlin reaches into his Jacket pocket and pulls out a bottle of Old Overholt Whiskey. The three men sit on the grass by the ditch and sip the whiskey straight from the bottle. Actually, Merlin and King Arthur sip and Walter gulps the fiery liquid.

Walter gets back into the Model T and asks Merlin if he will crank it for him.

He has to shut the car off when he stops because it is in low gear forward when both feet are off the shifter pedals. The car starts with one pull of the crank. Walter makes a "U" turn behind us and motions for us to follow him as we head toward the Noland place. Walter's car has no roof and the windshield is cracked. It cannot be called a convertible because it is just an open shell which can not be converted to anything else.

It is fascinating to watch Walter get into his car. He puts his good foot on the running board and straightens his right leg. He then grabs his wooden leg and throws it over the door. He then leans on the wooden leg and pulls his good leg in, plopping down on the rag covered box from which he drives the car.

I ask "How can Walter crank the car to start it if it is always in low gear with no one in it?"

Merlin describes the procedure which Walter uses to start the car since he first got it. Prior to getting the

Model T, Walter walked or hitched a ride wherever he went. A one legged man really needs to go somewhere if he is going to walk. He often made it only half way home and slept on the roadside after drinking most of the supplies he had gone for. He mostly hitched a ride in the back of a Model A or Studebaker pickup or on a farm wagon since he smelled badly discouraging most from offering him a ride in their fine cars. Walter had a jack welded to the driver's side of the car. He jacks the rear tire just off the ground, retards the spark, sets the throttle on a low setting and cranks the car. When it starts, the rear wheel turns slowly in the air until Walter gets in and presses the shift pedals to neutral and adjusts the spark until the engine is running smoothly. He then pulls a rope tied to the door handle and jack mechanism, dropping the rear tire to the ground so the car can propel itself.

Merlin says "Walter often leaves his feet off the shift pedals and the car moves forward at a fast walking speed. He is then free to drink and drive simultaneously. When he is driving erratically, he is moving so slowly that other motorists are able to steer clear of him and he has thus avoided serious auto accidents."

Merlin says "The only thing better than the Model T would be a horse and buggy because the horse will take you home even if you are asleep."

We arrive at Walter's shack and get out unloading the supplies we are delivering.

Guinevere asks "Where do you want the supplies and food placed?"

Walter says "It would be good to put it into the wardrobe so I can protect it from animals that might mess with it."

We all carry the boxes of canned goods to the indicated storage place. Guinevere then brings out a brown paper bag with a pie and a loaf of fresh bread in it.

She suggests "Let's all have a picnic in the yard."

It's clear to me that she doesn't want to stay inside the dirty hovel a minute longer than necessary.

Walter protests saying "I have no proper dishes or utensils."

Guinevere says "I thought of that and have forks and spoons and tin plates which you are to keep after the picnic."

When lunch is over, we get into the Buick and wait while Merlin and Walter have a long talk.

When Merlin finally gets into the car, he says "Walter needs to get his teeth fixed so he can chew food."

We all noticed that Walter is gaunt and thin. His skin is sallow and yellow from too much alcohol. I am surprised to hear that Walter is in his early fifties. I would have guessed him to be eighty or ninety.

We talk nonstop on the way home.

Mom says "I have never seen Dad drink before and he is a deacon."

Dad says "It is only my second or third drink and I doubt it will become a habit since whiskey tastes a lot like kerosene."

Merlin reminds Mom "Jesus was accused of being a winebibber and turned water to wine in his first recorded miracle."

Mom softens her critical attitude and says "This day's events were planned to bring kindness to an unfortunate child of God and the Old Overholt may have been the most convincing act of kindness though I would have never thought of it."

She orders everyone in the car to keep the shared whiskey a family secret as some in the ladies sewing circle wouldn't understand.

A meeting of the Round Table is schedule after supper so the day's events can be put in perspective. I have no heroic tales to recount. I have a lot of questions. Merlin is front and center. He fends off questions from Guinevere about Walter's poor life style choices and unhealthy surroundings.

He states "Walter is deeply unhappy and bitter over the unfair tragedy he has lived through. Instead of praising the beauty of roses, he curses the thorns."

Merlin reminds us that livestock was kept in the castles of Europe, including even Camelot.

Guinevere responds with the phrase, "Cleanliness is next to Godliness, like it says in the Bible."

King Arthur says "That is a Shakespearian quote rather than scriptural."

The dangers and merits of alcohol are discussed at length. We discuss the futility of warfare using Walter as the prime example of the suffering brought to innocent men by armed conflict.

I inquire "Is the great notched sword I brandish an evil force?"

Merlin states "Tools are neither good nor evil, but may be used in the service of either."

He reminds us of the terrible social and health problems Walter has suffered as a result of alcoholism, even as he defends his purchase of alcohol for Walter as an act of kindness.

This is heavy stuff for a five year old!

PETUNIA

I view myself as primary protector of the inhabitants of the Kingdom of Johnson. Most of the inhabitants have four legs. The royal family gets first consideration when it comes to my services. With the help of Merlin's magic, support by King Arthur and Guinevere, and tactical support of the armor bearers, I have a lot of excess capacity. I even help illegal immigrants like Blackie and the skunk family if they don't encroach on the rights of the naturalized citizens. The inhabitants are constantly changing through birth and death and sale and even serving as food on our table. I know this sounds cruel, but life is hard and we learn to deal with it.

Our oldest brood sow gives birth to 13 piglets. We would not ordinarily name the piglets until they develop special personality or physical features because one cannot be distinguished from the other excepting males and females have different features. There are eight males and five females in this particular brood. The fates of the males are sealed at birth. They will be castrated and butchered in the fall. Some of the meat will be cured in our smokehouse for our consumption and some sold to the coop for cash credit. The females have a fair chance of being raised as brood sows or being sold to another farm that needs brood sows if they have the right physical characteristics. The eight male piglets are castrated at 2 weeks of age and their fate is sealed. None will ever father a brood of little piglets. Four of the females are hearty, healthy specimens that have a fair chance of remaining on as brood sows on our farm or another.

Petunia is the fifth female piglet. She is named by me and the armor bearers the day after her birth. She is easy to identify as she is a runt. Runt piglets are normally destroyed at birth since they don't gain weight as well as the others and deprive the healthy siblings of nutrition. Even if nature is allowed to take its course, the runts seldom survive as their larger healthy siblings don't allow them to suckle. It is a real battle to get on a teat full of milk when there are more piglets than teats. Merlin and King Arthur are loathe to destroy Petunia since we formed a bond by naming her.

Petunia's fate is discussed after supper the day the male piglets are castrated. Merlin suggests it is more humane to destroy the runt than to let her suffer death by starvation at the hands of her sibling piglets. His argument falls on deaf ears. This is clearly a situation which requires bold intervention. I volunteer to hand raise Petunia. We often hand raise orphan calves and even kittens. Petunia is a bit different as she might be seen as a financial liability rather than opportunity. I see Petunia neither as financial asset nor liability, but rather as a weak natural citizen of the Kingdom who needs special protection. Out of kindness to me more than kindness to Petunia, I am given charge of Petunia.

I immediately go to the pig pen to rescue my new charge. Petunia is on top of the pile of piglets attempting unsuccessfully to find an open teat. The other piglets are already markedly larger than they were at birth while Petunia has not grown at all. She has barely been able to get enough milk to stay alive. I pick her off the pile of rooting piglets and carry her to the house. Guinevere and

Merlin prepare a cardboard box with some rags for Petunia. I get permission to get a jar of milk from the Milk house. Merlin suggests that I should stir in a bit of molasses for extra calories.

Petunia is hungry. She has no idea how to drink milk from a bowl and I have no baby bottle with which to simulate her natural source of milk. We have a quart jar with a large rubber nipple with which we occasionally feed a calf. The nipple on that contraption is nearly as large as Petunia. We have fed baby kittens with a medicine dropper.

It takes a lot of droppers full of milk to satisfy a hungry pig. A person does what he has to do. I spend a full hour after bedtime feeding petunia from the medicine dropper. I quit because I am tired, not because Petunia is satisfied. I am beginning to understand why a person who over eats is called a pig. I don't believe I can satisfy Petunia's appetite if I feed her from the medicine dropper continuously day and night. Before falling asleep, I realize I will have to get help with the job for which I volunteered.

I gather the armor bearers together before breakfast and show them how I am filling the dropper with the milk and molasses mixture by squeezing the rubber bulb on the top and releasing it with the dropper immersed in the milk, filling the dropper. It is important to have Petunia ready when the dropper is pulled from the supply jar so the milk doesn't run out before the dropper is placed in Petunia's mouth. Petunia doesn't know the dropper is empty and keeps trying to suck more milk from it after the milk is squeezed into her mouth. It is a wrestling match to get the dropper free for reloading.

190

The two youngest armor bearers are unable to handle the dropper, but four more feeders are added after the lessons are complete. The two youngest armor bearers offer to help hold Petunia during feeding, thus completing our feeding plans. Petunia doubles in size within one week of experiencing our intensive care. The medicine dropper can no longer supply the needed nutrition. We start experimenting with spoon feeding. Petunia makes such a mess trying to suckle the spoon that Guinevere says "You have to feed her outside."

Merlin says "You will have to get a five gallon bucket and a funnel to satisfy the greedy little runt."

She isn't even a runt any more. She is as large as her siblings. We put her back in the pig pen with her mom and brothers and sisters to see if she can now compete with them for food.

Petunia likes us better than her own family. She doesn't even try to suckle though she is easily big enough to compete for teat space. Petunia figures she should be fed rather than get her own food. She doesn't even seem to like being around pigs. She thinks she is a people. We bring Petunia back to her own box where she makes contented little squealing noises as she rolls around on her soft bed of rags. She stands with her forefeet on the edge of her box squealing for food.

We are stuck with a long term obligation. Petunia is able to transition from spoon feeding to eating from a bowl within a couple of weeks. She is getting so strong she can take the spoon away from an armor bearer who is slow in spooning in her dinner.

Petunia started out staying in her bed all of the time. When she wet on the rags, we would change them and wash out the dirty rags and replace them as needed. Now petunia only gets in her box to sleep and never wets in the box. We take her outside to feed her and she quickly learned to wet outside as well. We give her a bath in the sink every night before she goes to bed and she wets immediately when taken outside for feeding in the morning. Petunia loves her baths and runs to the bathroom door and pushes on the door with her snout whenever she sees someone who might bathe her. We have an old bristle scrub brush with which we scrub her. She loves to get scrubbed and petted and played with, but most of all she loves to eat. Petunia has never turned food down in her entire life except when she was placed with the brood sow and required to obtain the food herself.

We churn our own butter and sell some at the coop. This generates more buttermilk than Guinevere can use in her cooking, so we feed the excess to the pigs. Petunia prefers buttermilk to sweet milk. She even likes sour milk which we only produce by accident. Anything with molasses in it is gulped down like the nectar of the gods. Petunia can easily rejoin the other pigs now that she is eating everything, but she is a house pig. She requires her food be served in a bowl. She requires a soft bed in which to sleep. Petunia is a spoiled pig. Guinevere says Petunia has to go outside. What will people say if they hear we have a pig living in our house? I take petunia to the pig pen and prepare a soft straw bed in a corner for her.

Guinevere calls me earlier than usual before breakfast. "Petunia is at the porch door waiting to come in."

She pushed her way in the house earlier this morning when Merlin and King Arthur opened the door to begin milking chores. Not only has petunia escaped from the pig pen, She has let a bunch of other pigs out as well. We spend the rest of the morning pounding stakes in the ground to prevent Petunia and the other pigs from escaping again and the afternoon returning pig escapees to the pig pen. They actually came back by themselves at feeding time and we merely had to let them in through the gate. Petunia is the hardest one to return to the pig pen and she is now big enough that it takes a lot of effort by Merlin to force her back inside.

You guessed it. Petunia is waiting at the porch door to come in first thing the next morning. We try to confine her to the pig pen three more times and finally give up though we did keep her confined for two days one time. Petunia just doesn't like to hang out with pigs. She doesn't know she is a pig herself. We decide that it will be better to let Petunia wander around free than to keep rounding up the pigs she has helped escape from the pig pen. The rest of the pigs are happy to stay in their familiar pen where they are fed and housed unless Petunia is among them. Petunia spends all of her time trying to get out of the pen and is remarkably effective in doing so. If the other pigs get used to more freedom, we may have a real problem on our hands.

Merlin says "Petunia is just like Sir Lancelot. She doesn't recognize her own limitations so she has none."

Guinevere isn't going to let Petunia back in the house. We finally solve the problem of housing for Petunia by taking some boards off the front porch and making a soft bed under the porch. Petunia likes her new home where she isn't stuck with a bunch of pigs and can hang out with me when I am outside. I can often be found resting against Petunia outside the sand box prison recounting adventures of the past to the armor bearers. Petunia follows Merlin and King Arthur to the barn when they are doing their morning chores. They often carry scraps from recent meals as a treat for Petunia. Petunia is now larger than any of the litter. She is a good hundred and fifty pounds. Everyone in the Johnson Kingdom scratches Petunia's back and talks to her as she follows them around. Even Guinevere likes Petunia although she is embarrassed when someone outside the family mentions our house pig.

The male pigs and one of the female pigs have already been butchered when things come to a head with Petunia. She decides to get in the Buick with us on Sunday morning. King Arthur and Merlin get their Sunday clothes dirty trying to force Petunia back out of the car. She won't get out until we all get out of the car and go in the house. Merlin then coaxes her out of the car with a bowl of cold oatmeal left over from breakfast. By the time we resolve the problem, it is too late to go to church.

Guinevere frets over what she will tell the ladies when they ask why we missed church. She makes us all promise not to mention Petunia as part of the problem. Petunia's reign as pig princess is about to end. Merlin solves the problem to everyone's satisfaction. He and I will bring Petunia to Walter Noland as a gift.

Walter needs the company and Petunia is a lot cleaner house guest than his goats and sheep and chickens.

DRIVING WITH NO LICENSE

Merlin offers to bring an apple pie to Walter Noland. He asks me to ride along for company. My sword will offer protection on the journey. Walter brags about the best blueberry pie he has ever eaten to anyone he meets since we last visited him with groceries and pie. Guinevere is known to bake a fine pie as is testified by the preacher and other guests who stop by the Kingdom for a visit. If Guinevere has sufficient warning, a chicken or two will be in the oven and either pie or cake will mark the occasion. Walter's praise is far beyond the casual note that the pie is good. He is willing to bet no one on earth bakes a better pie than Guinevere.

Many of the older farm kids belong to 4-H clubs. The four H's are Head, Heart, Health, and Hands, suggesting that a complete farmer is smart, sensitive, prudent with lifestyle choices and works hard. The 4-H clubs sponsor a county fair every summer and all of the community participates in contests to see who has the best of everything from livestock to craft projects to garden and field produce to canned goods, sewing and prepared foods. It is the highest honor to be selected as a judge. All winners are actually selected by a panel of judges to avoid any suspicion of favoritism. Mom won the pie baking contest last year and every farm in the county has one or two ladies gunning for that title this year. It sure doesn't hurt to get a little advance reputation boost like that Walter is offering. I wonder if his praise doesn't have an underlying motive like obtaining competing pies from various sources.

Merlin actually likes Walter, while most who know Walter either actively disapprove of him or at least avoid contact when possible. I noticed that Guinevere didn't push to personally deliver the apple pie.

On the way to Walter's shack, Merlin said "Walter is actually kind hearted. He doesn't take care of himself because he disapproves of himself even more than others do. He doesn't change because he really thinks he doesn't deserve to be in better health and more successful than he already is. Walter drinks a lot of liquor so he can confirm to himself how bad he is and to forget that he ever had aspirations to be anything other than the town drunk."

I am beginning to see Walter as a needy person through Merlin's eyes. I understand that Merlin isn't his friend because he admires Walter's choices, but rather because he sees Walter as a fellow human being with a different set of flaws than the standard ones we all accept.

Merlin says "You will never meet anyone who doesn't know something you don't know."

He says "I learn more from Walter than from folk who follow a more ordinary lifestyle because Walter marches to the tune of a different drummer."

I picture Walter carrying a flag in front of a parade out of step with everyone else because of his awkward gait with the wooden leg. I don't know if it is a complement or not when Merlin says "You are my special friend because you march to a different drum than any of the kids I have ever met."

I picture myself in front of a drummer pounding on the drum so fast that I can't keep pace as I race ahead of the parade with my flag. I ask Merlin "How do we tune in to our drummers?"

He says "We just have to listen and go with the flow."

Puzzling stuff for sure!

The conversation brings us to Walter's shack and we park behind his Model T. Walter is asleep in a chair on the porch. He doesn't wake up until a goat nearly knocks his chair over trying to hide from the strange car that has arrived. Walter has been drinking already this morning if my sense of smell is correct. His words are a bit slurred as he greets us. He pushes the goat off the porch and invites us to sit with him a spell. There is only one other broken chair on the porch, so I sit on the step and Merlin settles in for a conversation.

He answers Walter's question about what brought us over by announcing that we are delivering an apple pie for his consideration. "Guinevere will appreciate any suggestion as to what might improve its quality."

This pie can't be improved and we all know it! It is a deep dish pie with a flower pattern cut into the top crust. Extra sugar and cinnamon are sprinkled on the crust to form eye candy and aroma that is exceptional. Guinevere can't just ask Walter to enhance her reputation as a pie baking artist, but she provided the perfect bribe to get the job done. Walter offers to cut the pie and share it with us, but Merlin insists that it is prepared for Walter alone.

Merlin says "The pie will be better as desert." He offers to prepare us a breakfast to share even though it is nearing noon and we already had a full breakfast back at the Johnson Kingdom.

Merlin brought a dozen eggs and a tin of butter to fry them with. He also has some fresh biscuits left over from breakfast. He lights a burner on the stove and melts butter in a greasy old cast iron frying pan wiped out with a piece of flower sack he carries in his pocket as a handkerchief. He opens the chest door where we stored groceries a couple of weeks ago. He notices that most of the canned goods and supplies are untouched. He carves a piece from the side of ham and puts it in the frying pan with the half dozen eggs cooking there.

Walter rummages around and finds the plates and utensils we left on our last visit. Merlin loads the plates up and wipes the frying pan clean with the flour sack handkerchief. We all return to the porch for a feast.

Merlin says to Walter "You seem to be getting a bit thin. Are you eating regularly?"

Walter says "I am having trouble eating since my visit to the dentist with you last week."

He got a set of false teeth after the old broken ones were extracted and the false teeth hurt him when he eats.

Merlin asks "Are you using the denture cream to hold your teeth in place?"

Walter says "I used the first tube up and haven't gotten any more."

Merlin inquires about other health matters as well. It is apparent that Walter isn't taking care of himself at all. He has a sore on the stump of his amputated leg, so he leaves the leg off a lot and then he can't get around very well.

Merlin offers to drive to Solen Springs where a few medicines are available at the gas station and general store. He will get salve for the sore on Walter's amputated leg and aspirin and denture cream. I offer to stay with Walter while Merlin runs the errands hoping to hear stories of Walter's past. Walter says I ask too many questions, but continues to answer them as fast as I can spit them out. He shows me how he keeps his wooden leg on by fastening it to straps attached to a belt under his shirt. He shows me how he starts the Model T by jacking up the rear wheel so it can turn without propelling the car forward when he cranks it. He shows me how he adjusts the spark, first retarding it so the car will start easily and not kick the crank back breaking his arm, and then advancing the spark to make the engine run smoother and faster. He jacks the car up and then pulls the release rope dropping the rear tire back on the ground.

Walter has few guests and he enjoys showing me how he does things. His goats are particularly interested in our activities and push up against us to get patted and noticed.

Walter offers to start the car for me and let me adjust the spark to get the engine running smooth. I stand on the rag covered box Walter uses as a drivers seat and signal that I am ready. The spark is retarded and the Model T fires up with one pull on the crank. I advance the spark carefully as Walter keeps recommending a bit more advance. Walter walks to the side of the car to better observe my action when a pesky goat seeking attention butts Walter right on his wooden leg. The straps are not tightened well and the leg falls off propelling Walter to the ground. He grabs at the side of the car to maintain his balance and grabs the trip rope to the jack.

The Model T rear tire drops to the ground and the car lurches forward in low gear with me at the wheel. My sword is on the floor beside me, but I can't reach it and it wouldn't do me any good if I could reach it. I steer the car onto the read so it won't hit anything and look back to see what happened to Walter. He is furiously trying to get his leg re-attached and push away the pesky goat that is still butting at him to get attention. He finally gets his leg re-attached and is on his feet as I am turning the corner in the road at four or five miles an hour. He is lost to my sight.

I never drove a car before. Steering is intuitive. I turn the steering wheel clockwise and the car turns right. I turn the wheel counterclockwise and the car turns left. I use the entire dirt roadway wobbling from right to left, managing to keep the car between the ditches on either side and I avoid hitting anything. My driving is starting to improve when I see Walter round the corner behind me waving his arms in the air with three goats following closely behind him. I am moving a bit faster than he is and we both know it. Walter falls to the roadway as he attempts to move faster and the goats push at him assuming he is playing with them.

Walter sits in the road with his goats as I disappear over a small hill. Sir Lancelot has never faced a dilemma like this before. He might talk to a runaway horse or pull

201

on the reins to stop it, but this automobile is another situation altogether. The cows wouldn't stop on command either and the result was an ignominious trip into an electric fence and a cow pie facial. The brake lever is down by the door on the left, but I have no idea how to work it. Two of the shifting pedals must be depressed to take the car out of low gear, but I am standing on a box far from those pedals. I cannot abandon my station at the steering wheel or the car will careen into the ditch and maybe turn over or hit something and get wrecked.

I decide that I will have to keep steering the car down the road until it runs out of gas. I wonder if it has enough gas to get to Illinois. After the initial shock of finding myself behind the wheel of a moving automobile and a bit of steering practice, I am actually beginning to enjoy myself. The big smile on my face evaporates as I see a dust cloud ahead which can only be an approaching car or truck. I begin to concentrate on keeping the car on the right side of the road as my heart races. Will we have a head on collision? What will I do if I get to a stop sign and there is oncoming traffic? I think I will be able to keep the car on the right side of the road to pass this oncoming vehicle, but there may be many more tests of my newfound driving skills ahead.

As the approaching car comes over a small rise in the road, I recognize our Buick. I steer carefully to the right side of the road as Merlin approaches. He slams on the brakes, and jumps out of the Buick as I pass him waving my hand in the air. He sprints behind the Model T and pulls himself into the car over the rear bumper. He leans over my shoulders and takes control of the steering wheel. I move to stand beside the rag covered box while

Merlin figures out how to work the shifting pedals and puts the car out of gear and pulls the brake handle. The car comes to a stop and my racing heart slows to a more ordinary rate. Merlin just sits on the rag covered box with his feet holding the shifting pedals in neutral. He looks at me for a long time without saying a word. He is breathing hard because he had to run really fast to catch me and climb in the car.

He finally asks. "Where are you going?"

"Illinois." I answer.

After another long pause, Merlin asks "Do you intend to stay in Illinois or will you be just passing through?"

We both laugh long and hard. Merlin drives the Model T to a place where he can turn it around and heads back to the Walter Noland place. We pass the Buick sitting in the road with the engine running and driver's door open and continue on to Walter's shack. Merlin parks the Model T in its place and leans forward to twist a switch on the dash and the engine quits. I could have done that if I had known what that switch did. Walter is sitting in the same chair we found him in when we first arrived. He is asleep again, rather, this time his is asleep and really drunk. A nearly empty whiskey bottle has slipped from his hand and is lying on the porch next to his chair.

Merlin says "The Buick is a couple of miles down the road and we had better get hiking to retrieve it."

He and I are in no special hurry to get to the car. We talk as we walk down the road like two equals. After all, we are both good drivers though I haven't had a lot of practice. Merlin asks me to tell him how I happened to be heading for Illinois in Walter's car. Things happened so fast I am a little confused about exactly how it happened. I explain the events as best I can recall them. Merlin asks pointed questions and I remember more details that I had forgotten to mention.

By the time we get to the Buick, the story is pretty complete. Merlin is chuckling under his breath all the way back to Walter's place. I am rethinking my heroic actions and planning a great meeting of the Round Table for the telling of the day's events. Everyone will have to be in costume for this celebration.

Walter is still asleep/drunk. Merlin places the sack of denture crème, aspirin, and the black bag balm (recommended by the pharmacist for Walters's leg sore) on the porch next to the sleeping derelict.

Merlin says "Let's not wake Walter before we leave. What will he think as he comes out of his drunken stupor? He will probably think he was hallucinating. But, then, what about the pie and medicines? Walter might swear off his liquor after he ponders these events a while."

We arrive home later in the afternoon than originally planned to be peppered by questions from Guinevere. "What does Walter think of the pie? Why did we take so long to deliver it? Why is Merlin wearing that big grin on his face? What have we been up to?"

We assure her that all of her questions will be answered at tonight's meeting of the Knights of the Round Table if everyone attends in full royal dress. They did. The questions were answered. I got another notch on my sword for heroism displayed in saving a helpless runaway automobile.

TO THE DUMP

Every farm in our community has a place where old junk is discarded. The junk pile is not a dump. Broken tools and machinery, tin cans, pieces of barbed wire and the like are stored here. Neighbors are allowed to dig through each others junk piles to find a piece they need for a repair job on the farm. It would be unpleasant to be digging through a junk pile looking for a bolt and get into a pile of rotten potatoes or apples. Items of this sort (garbage) are discarded at the county dump down on the North Range.

We take very few trips to the county dump as is the custom of most in our area. Garbage is usually incorporated into pig feed or recycled in some other way such as fertilizer. We know that animal entrails from butchering do not incorporate well into the manure pile as fertilizer since they tend to gum up the manure spreader and fly off in big chunks. Mom cut up entrails from hog butchering one year to bury with the sweet corn she planted and raccoons dug up all of her sweet corn.

King Arthur announces to the audience watching the hog butchering, "These tubs of offal will stink by morning. We will make a trip to the dump after milking tonight." (The entrails don't have to wait until morning to stink in my opinion.) The announcement is met with cheers. A trip to the dump is a special treat.

Merlin hooks the two wheeled trailer to the Buick and parks it near the table by the smoke house where the butchering has been in progress all day. He and King Arthur load three wash tubs full of hog innards onto the trailer. Washing down the butchering table, salting and wrapping the hams and starting a fire in the smoke house absorb all the time until milking.

I assemble the armor bearers for a planning session. "We will be facing great danger tonight at the dump. Bears rummage through the garbage. I will have the great notched sword to ward off any bear attacks. All of you will have to remain in the car with windows rolled up so I can protect you."

Marvin and Dennis chime in, "We want to bring a baby bear home to play with." The rest of the armor bearers immediately agree that a pet baby bear will be fun to play with in the sandbox prison. "He can stay in there at night so he won't wander off and get lost."

The rest of the afternoon is spent discussing ways to sneak a baby bear into the car without raising suspicion from Merlin, King Arthur and Guinevere. We decide to name our new pet "Bee Bee" (Baby Bear). Unfortunately, we focus more on our parent's reaction to our plans than on Mama Bear's response.

Merlin and King Arthur are in a jovial mood as they come in from milking. As they are washing up for supper, they discuss the upcoming trip to the dump. Merlin says, "Don't bring food to feed the bears. George Alford brought a few loaves of stale bread to feed the bears so his girlfriend, June Allison, could get a closer look at them. Two bears came over to the car and ate the bread he threw on the ground next to the car. He rolled the window up when they tried to see if he had more bread for them inside. June started screaming when the bears pushed on the car and then climbed onto the hood to look in the front window. The old Studebaker they were driving has a cloth roof. A bear climbed on top and began digging a hole in the roof to get at any bread they might be hoarding inside. George started the car and the bear on the hood jumped off in surprise. The bear digging on the roof was so busy trying to get in, that he kept on digging. Blowing the horn didn't distract him, so George drove off with the bear still on the roof. George turned hard from side to side and couldn't shake the bear off. He slammed on the brakes and popped the clutch. The bear finally jumped off the car three miles down the road. June saw enough bear that day for the rest of her life. She had laryngitis for a week from all the screaming she did. She had seen enough of George as well, since they never dated again."

We all laughed at Merlin's story. I said, "I would have poked that bear in the belly with my sword. I will bring my sword along tonight in case there is any trouble with the bears. The dump would be a good place to go to get rid of a pesky girlfriend."

Kenny asks, "Can baby bears hurt you? They look real cuddly. I would like to have a baby bear to play with. I would name him 'Bee Bee' for baby bear." He stopped talking when he realized that I and all of the other armor bearers were glaring at him.

The plan will be off if he asks if we can bring a baby bear home and permission is refused. It is better to do something you want to do and wait for people's response than ask permission and have to disobey if you do it anyway.

Guinevere saw what was going on and said, "You should let Kenny talk about his dreams. He is little and doesn't get to talk as much as you bigger kids."

She doesn't realize that he isn't talking about his dreams. He is exposing our plans. It does seem like she has some sympathy for those plans which is an encouraging development.

We all pile into the car for our trip to the dump as soon as supper is over. Guinevere says, "I will wash dishes when we get back. We should get to the dump while it is light so we can watch the bears a while."

On the way to the dump, it is traditional to sing, "To the dump, to the dump, to the dump, dump, dump;" to the tune of the William Tell Overture. We learned that from the introduction to the Lone Ranger on the radio every Tuesday night. We sing the opening line to the William Tell Overture all the way to the turnoff to the North Range.

Merlin says, "Let me teach you a poem!" He begins, "Fuzzy Wuzzy was a bear. Fuzzy Wuzzy had no hair. Fuzzy Wuzzy wasn't very fuzzy, was he?" We are all able to recite the entire poem by the time we arrive at the dump if we can keep from laughing in the middle of it. We always laugh at the end of it.

We aren't the only family that comes to the dump to watch black bears forage among the scraps discarded there. We see four cars parked at the upper end of the dump. They are watching a couple of black bears nosing around in the pile of waste. We back our trailer as far out onto the pile as it will go without getting the car wheels off the hard ground.

King Arthur says to Merlin, "I will sit at the wheel with the car running in case those bears get too curious about our load and you can dump the tubs off the back of the trailer. If you tell me to drive ahead, I will pull away from the bears with you riding in the trailer."

We have all of the windows down with as many heads as will fit in a window watching Merlin dump the refuse over the back of the trailer. The bears at the other end of the dump exhibit no interest whatever in our activities so the refuse is dumped without incident and the empty tubs are stacked upside down on the trailer. Merlin cleans his hands on the rag he tied to the trailer at home and climbs back into the car.

King Arthur asks, "Do you want to get a closer look at the bears?" The decision is loud and unanimous. Our enthusiasm makes the car rock. No one got into the car just to watch the garbage tubs get emptied or smell that unique smell of mixed garbage and trash. We are here to see the bears. Some of us are actually here to capture a bear. We drive down to the other end of the dump and

210

park between two cars already there. The two young strangers in the Pontiac both have their heads out the passenger window as they talk and point to the bears.

I tell them, "You can each have your own window to look out of." We have to take turns putting our heads out of our windows so we can see well because there are eight people in our car. They just smile and wave at me, ignoring the wisdom of my observation.

Guinevere laughs and says, "Its fun to share." as she hugs King Arthur while looking out the driver's window with him. "Oh, look!" she exclaims as she points behind the car. A mamma bear and two tiny cubs are coming out of the brush heading straight toward our trailer.

Kenny exclaims, "Its Bee Bee and his brother." Everyone laughs. All attention in the parked cars turns to watch this new development. Mamma bear lifts her nose high in the air checking out the most interesting odors. There are a lot of odors to be checked out for sure.

She likes the smell of our empty wash tubs and climbs halfway into the trailer pushing them around with her nose. The cubs climb in to investigate better. Mamma bear turns the tubs right side up and licks the inside of a tub. The cubs get into the tub and she pushes them out with her nose. This is the best dump bear show ever. Merlin says "Roll the windows up and watch through the back window."

The tubs are stacked together and mamma bear gets one out of the stack and drags it to the ground next to the trailer where she licks it clean. The cubs are inside the other tubs in the trailer. Mamma bear turns her attention to those tubs nosing the cubs away from her prize. They tumble about right beside the car wrestling with each other.

Mamma bear loses interest in the well cleaned tubs and heads for more interesting smells ahead. She walks between our car and the Pontiac ignoring the people inside. All windows are up, but noses are pressed to the glass. One cub on the other side of our car sees mamma bear pass the front of our car and clamber down into the pile of refuse. He scrambles after mamma bear leaving his playmate behind. Bee Bee is nosing at a beetle beside our back tire.

This is too good to be true. As King Arthur opens the drivers door to throw the tub back onto the trailer, Marvin, Dennis and I open the back door on the other side of the car and leap on top of the startled cub. Bee Bee lets out a squeal as we throw him onto the back seat of the car and pull the door shut. Merlin and Guinevere are watching the bears in front carefully to be sure they make no move toward the car while King Arthur is outside. They miss the back seat action entirely.

Mamma bear also missed the action, but she didn't miss the squeal of alarm from Bee Bee. She stands on her hind legs, looking toward us. Merlin shouts to King Arthur, "Get back in the car! That bear is upset with

212

you!" King Arthur leaps back into the car and closes the door as mamma bear starts toward the car.

Bee Bee is squealing and trying to get loose from his tormenters. He tears the back of the front seat with his claws trying to get loose. The front seat passengers, who had been distracted by the odd behavior of mamma bear, now realize that something is going on in the back seat. The family in the car beside us is pointing at our car and laughing. They watched the kidnapping of Bee Bee as it occurred.

Merlin leans over the seat back and spots Bee Bee under the pile of kids on the floor. He turns to King Arthur and shouts "Get out of here right now! The kids have a bear cub in the back seat."

King Arthur says, "What did you say?" He immediately starts the car and backs out of our parking spot. Mamma bear knows something happened to her cub, but can't figure out where he is. We stop when we are a couple hundred feet from the action. Merlin jumps out of the car and opens the back door. Bee Bee backs up against the far door and squeals louder. Merlin reaches in and grabs the little fellow by the back of the neck and hauls him out of the back seat.

Mamma bear bellows and charges toward us. Merlin jumps in the front seat and slams the door. We drive off as the bear family is reunited. Guinevere asks, "How did the bear get in to the car?" Merlin, watching the bears, says, "That is the way a mom should act if her child is in danger." King Arthur says, "Did you kids pick up any dynamite or anything else fun to play with while we were at the dump?" Kenny says, "I thought you said I could keep Bee Bee."

This adventure can't wait for a meeting of the Round Table for its telling. Everyone is talking at once all the way home although very little real information is exchanged. We forgot our poem about Fuzzy Wuzzy and didn't even sing "To the dump, to the dump, to the dump, dump, dump," until we are almost home.

Kenny asks, "Can we can visit Bee Bee next week?"

No one answers. I think people should listen to little kids more. It's surprising what they might learn.

WALTER TAKES A BATH

Walter Noland becomes the topic of several conversations after supper in the Johnson household. Guinevere insists that Merlin and I must visit him soon to explain how his car was returned so he can be at peace with his sanity. He may be a drunk. He may make unwise decisions about life style and health. He is not insane. Guinevere is afraid our prank of returning the car with no explanation may cause poor Walter to question his sanity. Who can predict what a man might do if he thinks he has lost his mind?

Merlin suggests that delivery of a jar of the prized choke cherry jelly might offer good excuse to visit Walter again. This suggestion nearly gets the trip cancelled as Guinevere has already decided who is to get a jar and for what occasion. Merlin adds that a fresh loaf of bread and a tin of home churned butter would be appropriate accompaniments to the jelly. Guinevere quickly agrees to the proposed gifts as she realizes that delay will cause her more work and treasure.

She says "You forgot to mention that soap and dish towels are needed at the Noland shack."

Merlin says "I will include those items even though Walter won't appreciate them like my first suggestions."

We are on our way back to Walter's shack with the gifts in a wooden apple crate in the trunk of the Buick.

I ask Merlin "Can I practice driving on the way?"

Merlin moves the seat back a little and slides me over onto his lap. He slows down to idle speed in low gear and we proceed down the road at ten miles an hour. I'm getting good at driving by now and keep the car on my side of the road with very little weaving within my lane of traffic. We even pass Floyd Anderson going the other way in his Studebaker pickup. He and Merlin exchange waves as they pass.

Merlin allows me to turn off County B onto the dirt road leading to Walter Noland's Shack. This road is narrow and I take my half out of the middle. No one is coming anyway and the only likely traffic would be Walter in his Model T which wouldn't be going much faster than we are.

Merlin says "I can relax a bit now that you are driving on a familiar road where you have driven in the past."

Merlin asks "Where is the turnoff to Illinois located?"

I tell him "I planned to watch for a sign but I'm not sure how to spell "Illinois" so I might have missed it.

He tells me "You could wind up in Minnesota by accident if you missed the turn south to Illinois."

Merlin asks "What is so attractive in Illinois since it is a really long drive that could take more than a full day."

I remind Merlin "You once told me of a humongus zoo in Chicago that has more animals than Noah had on the ark."

I catch him on that one! I ask "Where did the extra animals come from?"

Merlin is stumped.

216

I ask Merlin "Will you take me to the zoo?"

Merlin replies "The zoo will come and get you if they want you."

Merlin slides me out of his lap and resumes control of the car as we approach Walter's place. We pull in behind the Model T and shut the motor off as Walter waves to us from his chair on the porch. I wonder if he has moved since we left him there two weeks ago.

Walter asks "What occasions your visit?"

Merlin says "We have a few more groceries for your consideration. Are you eating better?"

Walter says "I am getting so fat and lazy from eating pie and the other good food that I think it might harm my health.

Merlin asks "What health?"

Walter gets serious at this point and asks Merlin "Do you think I might die soon?"

Merlin tries to lighten it up a bit with his reply. He says "I called the County Clerk to check on that and he says there is no expiration date on your birth certificate."

Walter won't be distracted by humor. He presses Merlin explaining why he is concerned with questions about his health. He admits "I drink too much." He admits "I don't eat very well." He admits "I don't keep the place up." (Implying that he isn't very clean.) He says "I figure I don't need baths any more than my goats and chickens. They never brush their teeth or wash their hands before eating. They don't seem to care if they are eating out of clean dishes."

After explaining why he doesn't take care of himself, he then admits "That argument doesn't hold water."

He looks at his goats and chickens and sheep and realizes that they wouldn't live as long as they do if he wasn't taking care of them. Even so, they only live a few years. None of his animals is as old as he is.

Walter then asks Merlin directly, "Do you think I am going to die?"

Merlin looks at me like I should answer the question. I know the answer.

I look straight at Walter and say "Of course you are going to die! We are all going to die! You'll die sooner if you don't take better care of yourself, but none of us knows when we are going to die. That is in God's hands."

Walter looks at Merlin and says "If all of my friends spoke truth to me like your nephew, I might be a better man."

Merlin responds "I know for a fact that you are a good man."

He says "Some of your friends might be criticizing you for minor flaws while they hide larger flaws of their own."

This is the first time I am included in an adult conversation as an equal. I am more commonly viewed as entertainment by a group of adults. That fact never escapes my notice.

Walter again turns to me and asks, "What do you think will happen to me when I die?"

218

It seems that I have been ordered to be truthful instead of kind. I look at the ground a bit and then lock eyes with Walter. "Mom says you will go to Hell if you don't get saved and baptized. I think the preacher thinks the same if I understand his sermons rightly."

Merlin isn't helping me out a bit. He seems to be studying the activity of a beetle crawling around on the porch. This is a pretty tough conversation for a kid. I don't feel like Sir Lancelot today. He would have answers to any question on the table.

Walter says, "What do you think?"

What do I think? Is my thought more important than the references I just gave? I don't know what I think! I have to think about that a while. I'm not even sure what Merlin thinks. He is usually a lot easier on Walter than any of the other adults I have heard discussing Walter.

This answer has to be right. I finally say, "I think you better do it just to be safe. I wouldn't want you to go to Hell. You've had a hard enough time right here on this earth."

I look at Merlin to see if I got it right. Merlin is still studying the beetle.

Walter asks Merlin, "Will you take me over to the preacher's house so I can get a few things straightened out?"

Merlin says, "I will do whatever you want."

We all pile in the front seat of the Buick, me in the middle.

Merlin asks Walter, "Would you rather go by yourself?"

Walter says, "I might neglect to do what I have to do if I put it off."

We head to the preacher's house.

On the way, Walter says, "I really need you to come with me to be sure I don't chicken out and to be sure I do it right." He admits that he has cast a few dispersions on the preacher's behavior at times but he didn't really mean it. He's not even sure the preacher will talk to him if we aren't with him.

Merlin and I sit in the Buick while Walter knocks on the parsonage door. He and the preacher disappear inside. I remind Merlin that we forgot to give Walter his jelly and bread and soap and dishtowels as we wait.

Merlin says, "I forgot all about that stuff when you went to preaching to Walter."

I defend myself vigorously. "It is you who brought up Walter's health. It is Walter who wants to know about dying. I was stuck in the middle and just tried to be honest when you hesitated to answer his questions. I still don't know the right answer. Did I mislead Walter?"

Merlin says, "Walter has heard the same story from everyone who ever brought him stuff or tried to help him out. Walter never paid any attention before. Maybe Walter has been looking for an excuse to do this for a long time and you just gave him the excuse he needs."

I feel a little less responsible for whatever is going on in the parsonage right now.

Walter comes out of the parsonage with a giant grin on his face. The preacher is right behind him and they both wave to us in the car. The preacher reaches out and slaps Walter on the back in congratulation just as Walter is stepping off the porch. Walter misses his step and sprawls out on the path. He didn't bring his walking stick with him on this trip.

Merlin jumps out of the car and he and the preacher help Walter to his feet. They all shake hands and then the preacher comes to the car and shakes my hand. I'm being treated as an equal by everyone today. I feel more comfortable as Sir Lancelot who has a reputation to stand on.

Merlin tells Walter about the gifts in the trunk of the Buick on the way back to the shack.

Walter says "I appreciate the food, but the gift you gave me today is much better. You brought me HOPE."

Merlin listens as Walter goes on and on about how happy he is to be going to Heaven although he hopes to put it off for a while. He announces that he has already made plans to be baptized next Sunday morning. Wow! Things are happening so fast I can hardly keep up.

We drop Walter off at his house and bring in the gifts Guinevere sent. Walter is talking nonstop and we forget entirely about the purpose of our trip. We finally leave without explaining how Walter's car was returned to him.

Merlin says, "I have known Walter for thirty years and Walter hasn't talked this much that entire time prior to today."

We arrive home, again much later than expected. Guinevere plies us with questions. "What do we do all day when we visit Walter? Did Walter like the stuff she sent? What did he say when we explained how his car was returned? Was he drunk again? Is he still losing weight?"

We admit, "We forgot to tell Walter how his car was returned."

We trigger another avalanche of questions when we say that Walter got saved today and will be baptized next Sunday if he doesn't change his mind before then.

NEXT SUNDAY:

Every member of our little church is in attendance today. The news that Walter Noland is going to be baptized spread through the community faster than the news of the start of WW II. A couple of bartenders are in church for the first time to see if their business is in jeopardy.

The deacons took the cover off the baptismal tank under the pulpit and filled it with water prior to the service. The preacher has to stand at a lectern in front of the first row of pews for the preaching service where he gives the longest and most energetic sermon of his life. This is the first time he ever got to preach to a packed house. The pews are full and several people are standing in back to witness this most unexpected event.

Finally, the baptism of Walter Noland is announced. A Wire has been strung across the platform behind baptismal tank where Walter will be able to change into dry clothes after the baptism. The wire is held by two eye screws fastened to the walls on either side of the platform. A sheet is hung over the wire to form the changing room. Everything is ready.

The preacher steps behind the curtain and steps out holding Walter Noland by the hand. Walter leans his walking stick against the wall and climbs down into the cold water with a lot of assistance from the pastor. The preacher introduces Walter and preaches another sermon with Walter shivering in the cold water. He then asks Walter a whole series of questions to be sure Walter realizes what a great decision he has made. Walter's teeth are chattering from the cold and he has to push them back in a couple of time because he is out of denture crème again. He merely nods his head in assent to each question as he is shivering too violently to speak and he may lose his teeth if he opens his mouth.

Finally, satisfied that nothing more can be said about baptism, the preacher puts his handkerchief over Walter's mouth and nose and leans him back into the cold water. Walter's wooden leg floats to the surface and he cannot get it back under him. He flails about, splashing water all the way to the third pew of the church. He pulls the pastor under water by his tie in an attempt to get a breath of air. The cold water causes two parishioners to scream in surprise spoiling the solemnity of the sacrament. The preacher pulls his face from the water and holds Walter's head above water while Walter struggles to get his wooden leg back under himself.

The two finally make their way back up the steps and Walter grasps his walking stick and disappears behind the sheet divider. The preacher starts singing a hymn and the congregation joins in, almost rescuing the baptismal service from disaster.

Slosh. The sound of a wet shirt hitting the floor is heard from behind the sheet. Next comes a profanity. Then, a loud "TWANG" as the eyebolts are jerked from the walls and the wire and sheet collapse onto the platform floor with Walter tangled in them. His britches are around his ankles and there are no clothes above his ankles. Walter gathers the sheet around him as the preacher shouts out that the service is dismissed.

We discuss the service on the way home from church. Guinevere asks if the profanity she heard cancels Walter's conversion.

Merlin says "That profanity may have been justified under the circumstances."

I'm hoping God isn't mad at me for getting Walter into this predicament.

King Arthur wonders if Walter should be baptized again to be sure it is done right.

We all agree that neither the preacher nor Walter will likely agree to schedule a second attempt.

Walter hasn't been back to church since his baptism. I'm still not sure if he is going to heaven or not. He at least gave it a yeoman's try.

GROOM

I looked this word up in the Merriam-Webster Dictionary to be sure I was using it correctly in defense of my actions. As a verb, "groom" may mean "to clean and care for", or it may mean "to make neat or attractive". You can easily see that one who grooms another has the best intentions. I really did mean well.

We are looking for new off-site egg nests in the machine shed. The youngest armor bearer calls us together to see her new discovery. She hasn't found another nest full of eggs. She found a strange device with an electric cord attached to it. It is at the bottom of an old wooden box covered with dust and debris. No one has any idea what this thing might be, but it looks like it might be important. We head for the house with the strange gadget and our basket half full of eggs collected during our morning hunt. I think we may have discovered an important lost piece of equipment.

We get a rag from the cleaning supplies and wipe the dust from our find. There is an air of anticipation as we contemplate a possible reward or at least a bit of praise for discovering the lost gizmo.

Guinevere looks at the object we carried in with the eggs and asks "What is it?"

It seems to be a heavy black tube with an electrical cord sticking out of one end. It is placed on top of the wood box to be inspected by King Arthur and Merlin when they finish milking and come in for breakfast. It must do something or you wouldn't have to plug it in.

We can't wait to find out what it does and why it was neglected in an old box in the corner of the machine shed. It might be some sort of magic generator or noise maker or light or have some other mysterious function.

Merlin comes in from milking and exclaims "The coffee smells great!" as he removes his barn boots and bends over the sink to wash his hands.

King Arthur bends over to remove his boots and glimpses our discovery sitting on the wood box. He says, "What's this?" as he picks it up.

Our first thought is that he doesn't know what it is either.

His next remark clears that up when he says, "I haven't seen these shears since we gave up trying to make a few bucks raising sheep for their wool. Where were they found? How did they get here? I wonder if they still work."

He twists the black plastic tube and the end of it comes off revealing a row of tiny sharp teeth. He walks over to the electrical outlet by the kitchen door and plugs it in. The shears make a quiet buzzing sound when he pushes the switch on the handle. They don't appear to be doing anything. He places the shiny metal part on his forearm and moves the shears up his arm leaving a trail of bare skin where arm hair used to be.

He says, "These shears have weathered time well. They are as sharp as they were when we last used them to shear our sheep. I wonder if anyone can use them? Only a few neighbors raise sheep. We might leave them at the co-op to see if we can sell them or trade them for something."

He asks "Where did you find the shears?"

He nods understanding when we describe the old wooden box in the corner of the machine shed. He commends us for bringing the shears to his attention as they have value to anyone who shears sheep.

He says" These heavy duty shears are fairly costly and should be returned to useful service."

He then unplugs the shears, places the cap over the cutting head and places it on the shelf behind the wood box.

We sit down to a wonderful breakfast of pancakes and bacon and hot syrup poured over a glob of butter in the middle of the pancake. Mom makes the syrup by stirring molasses and corn syrup and brown sugar together in a small pan on the stove. She adds just enough water so it will pour from the syrup pitcher and still stay mostly on top of the pancakes.

Merlin explains "It is impossible to eat pancakes without syrup. The syrup lubricates the pancakes so you can swallow them."

I used to think the syrup was just there to make the pancakes taste better. Mom can make eggs that have soft yolks and firm white part with no fringe on the edges. They taste wonderful with the pancakes and bacon and butter and syrup. The older folks wash this feast down with hot coffee, but the rest of us get milk to satisfy our thirst and complement the meal. The only trouble with this breakfast is that it tastes so good that you eat too much and your stomach can hurt afterward.

Merlin says "I don't just eat until I am full when we have pancakes. I eat until I am tired!"

I don't know how Mom can eat just one pancake when even the smallest armor bearer can eat at least two and Merlin may eat five.

The sheep shears are forgotten during the breakfast conversation where discussion centers on the Herford heifer that will be having her first calf most any time now.

King Arthur says "I think the calf will be marked with splotches like the Holsteins only they will be red instead of black because she was bred to a Holstein bull."

The conversation includes a lot of strange words like dominant and recessive genes and other things that cause animals to be like they are.

Merlin says "The same idea applies to people and that is why all of us have blonde hair and blue eyes."

I don't understand the connection between us and Holsteins and Herefords, but a lot of grownup talk is mostly nonsense.

At naptime I remember the sheep shears and King Arthur's arm hair. I bet they could be used to give haircuts. We get hair cuts when our hair gets so long it falls in our eyes. Mr. Jacobson has each of us sit on a tall stool at his house with a towel around our necks when it is time for haircuts. The whole evening is spent with the Jacobson family when we get our hair cuts. Mr. Jacobson says his father taught him to cut hair many years ago and he has perfected the art with years of practice. We all look alike after the haircuts. Our hair falls in a straight line across our foreheads and the line

228

follows around to the back just above the ears forming an upside down hair bowl appearance. Mr. Jacobson says it is important to leave plenty of hair on the crown of the head so a cowlick can't stand up making us look funny. It is hard to sit still while he is fussing around with the clippers and scissors so the edge of the hair bowl sometimes gets a bit ragged due to fidgeting.

We always bring special canned goods and a couple dozen eggs to compensate Mr. Jacobson. He talks continuously while cutting hair. He even stops cutting and waves his scissors around as he makes a point in the one sided conversation. Mom and Mrs. Jacobson spend the evening catching up on news about all the neighbors.

The more I look at the shears lying on the shelf behind the wood box, the more I think I can give haircuts better than Mr. Jacobson. He has clippers that cut by squeezing the handles together and releasing them. If he moves them through your hair when he isn't squeezing the handles together, it pulls your hair. The electric sheep shears wouldn't pull your hair and wouldn't require large hands to operate them. They cut the hair on King Arthur's arm effortlessly.

I decide to start my barber training at naptime tomorrow. We sleep as long as we want for our naps and then come downstairs by ourselves when we wake up. I am often the first awake and might wake up others so we can talk and plan stuff until everyone is awake and ready to head for the sandbox prison.

I bring the sheep shears to our bedroom after supper without asking permission since I really want to try out my idea. Asking permission could result in an unfavorable response. I will be careful not to damage the sheep shears so it should be ok. I don't see any disobedience or disloyalty in this stealthy approach.

Today is the first time in a long while that I am anxious for nap time to arrive. I don't dawdle over lunch or protest a bit at the instruction to take a nap. Tucked in with an embarrassing kiss, I lay awake planning to surprise everyone with my skill as a barber. I paid a lot of attention to Mr. Jacobson last time we had our hair cut. He emphasized that the most important thing is to get the hair cut evenly. If a bit too much is cut off one side, it can be easily corrected by cutting the same amount from the other side.

Guinevere is no sooner down the stairs to clean up the dinner dishes than I leap from bed and open the bottom drawer of the dresser where the shears are waiting. I figure I can cut some hair before some fall asleep and finish the others when they awaken from their naps. I confer with my older brother before he falls asleep. He is skeptical about my skill as a barber, but is fascinated when I plug in the shears and turn them on. They quietly buzz creating interest from another slow to sleep napster. I agree to let my older brother cut my hair when I am done with his in order to get his participation in the project. This is no problem as I need a haircut as much as he does and it would not be fitting to have everyone but me with a nice haircut. We don't have a tall stool, but I can't reach anyone's head seated on a tall stool anyway.

A pillow case is wrapped around my brother's neck as he sits cross-legged on the floor. The neck wrapping will keep hair from going down his neck. This is really proceeding well. I turn on the shears and start across the front of his head to create the reference line that will extend around to the back. I am having trouble getting a straight line because he keeps trying to turn his head to watch me. I tell him to bend his head forward and shut his eyes so I can start at the back where he can't try to watch me.

As I touch his neck with the buzzing shears he jerks his head back and says, "That tickles!" I have a strip of bare skin from behind his left ear all the way up to the crown of his head. I don't panic. I study the bare spot a bit and move to the right side of his head creating a symmetrical bare spot a bit higher than I planned. I return to the other side and attempt to even out the cut. My brother turns his head to tell me he thinks I am cutting his hair too high. The result of that movement is a bare spot from the crown of his head to the right ear. Now I have a problem. If I even this cut up, he will be bald from the middle of his head back. You guessed it. We finish the haircut with perfect symmetry but all of the hair is gone. My brother is bald.

He rubs his hands over his bare head and says, "The haircut feels funny".

I promised he could cut my hair so I wrap the pillowcase around my neck and sit cross-legged on the floor. My brother makes no attempt to cut my hair in the accepted pattern. His first cut is straight up the middle, front to back. I perceive this as childish vengeance for his bad hair cut. I was trying to do a good job but he messed it up by moving his head. Now he is intentionally cutting all my hair off. We stand facing each other after he is finished. I rub my bald head finding the feeling interesting. We start to laugh. This is really fun. Within twenty minutes, there are seven bald kids back in bed giggling instead of sleeping.

We march downstairs together since no one is asleep anyway. Guinevere has her back to us washing the last of the pots from dinner and remarks that our naps didn't last very long today. She turns to say something but whatever she was about to say gets lost in a scream. She pulls her apron to her mouth and stares at us.

We don't know what to say. I think she didn't recognize us and mistook us for strange goblins at first sight. We do look a lot different bald.

I speak up. "We won't have to go to Mr. Jacobson for haircuts any more since I am practicing giving haircuts."

It seems that Mr. Jacobson might get a vacation from cutting hair for a while because we don't have any hair to cut at present. Mom is worried about what the neighbors are going to say at church next Sunday.

When I tell her "We can wear hats and no one will know the difference, she starts laughing."

I ask if she would like me to give her a haircut and she shrieks with laughter. I think that means "no".

She tells us "Don't mention your haircuts to King Arthur and Merlin. They may not notice." Then she laughs again.

I hate to suggest it, but I think Guinevere is having a nervous breakdown.

I think my grooming days are over!

232

KIDS LIKE BALD

We are the talk of the town Sunday morning. This is the first time anyone outside of the Kingdom of Johnson has seen our haircuts. Guinevere is outraged at the implied suggestion when several ladies ask if our heads are shaved to get rid of lice. Guinevere took the question as an insulting suggestion that we may not be clean people. I mentioned before that one of her favorite Bible passages says "Cleanliness is next to Godliness." She insists that it is in there somewhere even though Merlin laughs and says that is a quote from William Shakespeare.

William Shakespeare might have written some of the Bible because he uses a lot of flowery language like the Bible does. Our Preacher says God wrote the Bible himself, but He had people who know how to write help him because He can't write even though he knows everything. It seems like He mostly used King James to write the hard stuff and a bunch of other guys are trying to write it better without the flowery language and they are getting it all mixed up.

We are easy to spot in church because of our bald heads. Grandpa Jorgenson is the only other bald person here today. All of the other kids envy our notoriety and spectacular change in appearance. We could have come to Church in tuxedos and a limousine without causing any more comment.

The girls are a bit less enthusiastic about the girl's haircuts, though they are enthralled with the look of the bald boys. They complain that it might be hard to tell girls from boys if everyone is bald and no girl would want to be mistaken for a boy.

I point out "Boys don't wear dresses and that is a plenty good differentiating tool."

They say "Girls should be able to put pretty pins and curls in their hair and braid it and do all sorts of other fancy things to make them look nice."

I point out "One can draw pictures on a bald head if she wishes to change her appearance."

That brings up the word "phew" in a context other than odors. I guess some ideas do stink.

I suggest, "Pretty hats with bows and flowers will also work!"

My two bald female armor bearers are about to cry. This comment brings their spirits back to the normal happy girl level.

I don't often get caught up in girl talk after church because girls aren't interested in danger and adventures and all the fun things in life. I really don't know what interests them because the girls never sit in a group and listen to my tales like the guys do. Today is different. Everyone seems to be interested in haircuts. Even the grownups are talking of nothing else. The adults seem more interested in why we decided to cut our hair off than how we did it. The kids all want to know how to get such a fashionable haircut. No one else has sheep shears. I speculate that the same result might be obtained with scissors. No one even considers shaving equipment as we have been warned never to touch those straight razors or important parts of our bodies will be amputated. Even

King Arthur and Merlin often cut themselves with those dangerous sharp implements.

Monday morning is here and we are off to school on the bus. My haircut and that of my brother are again the only topic of discussion. We are famous! Several classmates got wind of our haircuts from their parents talking to someone who saw us at church. They all rub our bald heads to feel the short fuzzy hair left. It is an interesting feeling. Tony Kisslick is the third student to be picked up after us and he is bald. We talked a lot after church yesterday and he said he was going to cut his hair but we weren't to tell anyone.

He climbs on the bus and waves to us wearing a silly grin. Everyone on the bus cheers as he walks to the back of the bus to sit by me and tell me how he obtained his haircut. He did it himself with his mom's sewing scissors. He showed the result to his parents proudly and his dad said a swear word that deacons shouldn't say. Tony didn't even dare to say the word to let me know what it was, but I can tell it was a really bad word. His mom got mad at his dad for using that word in front of Tony and made his dad fix up the haircut by soaping his head and shaving it with his straight razor where Tony had left little tufts of hair.

Tony's head is as smooth as glass. It feels different than my head because our shears left tiny short hairs. I think I will ask Merlin to shave my head with shaving cream and razor after my next haircut. Everyone on the bus has to feel my head and compare it to Tony's head after his entrance.

My head is rubbed so much by curious classmates over the next week that I'm not sure if the hair will ever grow back. If you walk across the yard in the same place often enough, the grass quits growing there and you make a path. I bet that why some old people are bald. They are probably puzzled a lot and rub their heads while they are thinking. After a long time, they quit growing hair where they rub it too much.

I guess ladies don't think as much, so they don't rub their hair off. I know that worrying will turn your hair grey! Kids don't worry much. I have never seen a grey headed kid yet. There might be some out there, but I've never met them. I think old people worry a lot because many of them are grey. They ought to worry. You can die for getting too old. I have decided that I'm not going to get old. I think that's what happened to my friend Walter Noland.

Every day, two or three more classmates come to school bald. Several of them actually talked their parents into cutting their hair off. Most of them got into some sort of trouble for doing it themselves without asking permission. I'm beginning to like the bald look.

Mr. Jacobson used his shears to cut Roger Lawson's hair nearly as short as mine. He calls it a butch haircut and says he used to cut hair that way a long time ago. I think he made that up to take credit for my invention. Anyway, I'm now famous for something other than being a Knight of the Round Table.

The new look hasn't caught on with the girls yet. It will probably spread to them when they realize how easy it is to wash your hair when you don't have any. I hate washing my hair because I always get soap in my eyes

236

and that hurts a lot. It also hurts to get your hair combed for church when it is real tangled up. When mom is in a hurry getting us ready for church, she pulls our hair with the comb pretty bad. She is a lot easier on hair combing for school because God won't be looking us over so close there. Someone pulled Sam's hair yesterday when they were scrapping and I realized that I don't have to worry about that any more as well. You must be getting the point by now. Bald is beautiful! All upside! No downside! The girls are just a bit slow to adapt new ideas but they will probably come around before long. All the cool guys in our school are bald and the rest envy us for having such understanding parents.

The teacher says the bald look is just a fad and will change again. I don't see why positive change won't last forever. People didn't get tired of cars and go back to driving horses when that fad started. I think a study of history would give the teacher a better perspective.

A HERO DIES

Jasper Inkvest, our mailman, usually leaves the mail in the box at the end of the driveway. Today, he brings the mail to the house and stands on the porch talking to Guinevere, Queen of the Kingdom of Johnson. Merlin notices the special mail delivery and walks back to the house to inquire about the mail. It might be a package of repair parts for the milk separator he ordered three weeks ago. Jasper is sitting on the porch steps and Merlin hunkers down beside him to chat. The armor bearers and I put the last of the eggs in the basket and hurry to the house to check out our visitor.

Jasper says "I noticed Walter Noland's Model T parked in the field just past the turnoff onto the dirt road leading to the Noland shack. I thought nothing of it yesterday, but the car is still sitting in the same place when I passed by again today."

Merlin scratches his head and remarks "Walter wouldn't leave his car there for two days unless he had car trouble or ran out of gas. Even at that, Walter is resourceful and would have returned with a can of gas after walking home, or he would have hitched up George, the ancient mule he keeps around for company more than for work. George can pull the car home easily enough and Walter isn't one to ask for help. He usually refuses help even when it is offered."

It is a dreary day today with low clouds and a cool mist in the air even though it is early September. Corn cutting and shocking for silage will be unpleasant in the damp weather. Merlin goes to the milk house where he

238

discusses the news about Walter's car with King Arthur. I tag along to keep informed. Walter and I are special friends after I got him to get saved and baptized this summer.

He says "I appreciate the gift of Petunia as she keeps me good company and she reminds me of you." What? I take that as a compliment though it is a bit questionable.

In just a few words, the rulers of the Kingdom of Johnson have a plan for the day. King Arthur will proceed to the cornfield with the small tractor to operate the corn binder which cuts the corn stalk just above the roots and ties them into bundles which are ejected onto the ground. Normally, Merlin would follow along behind standing the bundles into piles leaning against each other to stay dry until they are chopped and blown into the silo. Sometimes, Guinevere will drive the tractor and corn binder and both Merlin and King Arthur walk along stacking the corn bundles into shocks. Since the bundles are already wet, Merlin and Arthur will shock the corn tomorrow when the sun is out and handling the corn will be more pleasant.

Merlin will take the Buick out to Walter Noland's place to check on him. He asks me I want to come along.

I raise my sword high and exclaim "I am ready to assist Walter in any way needed. I will put the armor bearers in charge of guarding the Kingdom in my absence." We head for the house to get a loaf of fresh bread for Walter and let everyone know our plan.

I stand in front of the porch with the great notched sword held high. The armor bearers are seated on the porch listening with great attention as I describe the need for their vigilance during my absence. Ken asks if he can use my sword while I am gone, but I explain that the magical powers conferred by Merlin only apply to me. We walk to the apple orchard where we break a limb off of the dead crab apple tree and peel the bark from it fashioning a fine spear which will be the only weapon available in event of an emergency. Merlin comes out of the house with the loaf of bread intended for lunch wrapped in a towel. He and I walk to the car on our rescue mission.

I like riding along with Merlin because he talks to me just like he would to any adult. When he asks me a question, he waits for my answer as if it is important. He points out interesting things on the way and tells me of their significance. A lot of other adults treat me like a little kid. We speculate about the possibilities which might have occasioned Walter to leave his car at the roadside. Merlin suggests a lot of silly ones and we laugh together about them. I come up with the best one of all. Maybe Walter saw a pretty girl on the side of the road and got out to take a long walk with her. Then he got lost and couldn't find his car when she went home. I remember dreaming that it would be nice to take a long walk with Violet.

Merlin laughed so hard about that idea that tears came to his eyes and he had to slow down so he wouldn't steer into the ditch. Our trip seemed just started when we got to the turnoff toward Walter's shack. Sure enough! There is his car parked way off the road in a hayfield that already had its second cutting. We decide to look in the car to see if there are any clues as to why Walter abandoned it two miles from home. I offer to drive it back to Walter's shack if Merlin starts it for me. Merlin suggests that it will be better to get Walter and let him drive it home instead.

We stop our chatter as we approach the car. I can tell that Merlin is worried. Merlin reaches the car a step ahead of me and looks inside. He exclaims "Oh! No!" He leans his head on the side of the car. I climb up on the running board and look in.

Walter is lying on his back with his feet on the box from which he pilots the vehicle. His face is a mottled blue color and he is not moving. Petunia is stretched out next to Walter as if to provide him warmth and comfort. Merlin reaches out and places his hand on my shoulders as I come to grips with the information my eyes bring me even as my mind rejects the reality of it all. Walter Noland is dead. I am glad Petunia was there so he didn't have to die alone. We stand by the car in silence for a long time.

Merlin says "We should bring Petunia home so she can get some food and water."

We put Petunia in the back seat of the Buick and continue on to Walter's shack where Petunia is greeted by two goats as she pushes her way to the water trough.

Merlin pats Petunia on the back and says "Your duty is done. We'll take care of Walter for you."

We drive slowly back to Walter's car and Merlin lifts Walter out of the Model T and gently lays him on the back seat of the Buick. He opens the trunk and gets out a blanket to cover Walter's body. We roll down the windows even though there is a chill in the air because

Walter's poor hygiene combined with a bit of time since his death have created a strange odor which I shall always associate with death. We drive towards Superior, stopping at the parsonage to let the pastor know of Walter's passing. We then continue on to the funeral home in Superior where a somber faced man nods continuously while Merlin describes the details of Walter's death. He asks Merlin to come back after notifying the coroner of Walter's death so he can get more information about funeral arrangements.

We return to the mortuary and are ushered into a small room with low lights and lots of curtains on the wall. Merlin fills out a bunch of papers and selects a beautiful pine covered coffin with white silk lining. The bottom of the coffin rises up when the top is opened. I look at all the other choices with their brass handles and dark shiny finishes. I think Walter would like the one we selected best. I wonder what they did with Walter. He was wheeled into the mortuary on a steel stretcher with a black pad on it when we lifted him out of the Buick. Merlin had covered him again with the blanket from our trunk.

We drive home in silence.

King Arthur stopped cutting corn bundles and came into the house when Merlin went out to give him the news of Walter's death. Guinevere sat at the kitchen table across from Arthur holding his hands in hers. Grief is enveloping our house. I went out to the sandbox prison and told the armor bearers about Walter. I told them that Petunia had been with him when he died and stayed to protect him until we arrived. We are all sitting silently, not digging in the sand or telling stories or laughing and

242

shoving each other when Guinevere came to release the prisoners from the sand box prison.

Spaghetti with tomato sauce and hot dog pieces stirred into the sauce would normally have everyone in a jolly mood. No one sucks a long piece of spaghetti into his mouth flipping sauce onto his face as is the custom with such food. No one asks for seconds even though a fresh loaf of hot bread and butter are served with the spaghetti. The milking is in progress as Guinevere calls all of the neighbors with the sad news. They are in agreement that Walter's funeral will be held Sunday morning in place of the regular service.

We hold a meeting of the Round Table with Merlin leading the discussion. The army must be notified of the death of a distinguished WWI veteran. Walter's animals must be found new homes.

King Arthur says "Walter must be buried in the suit I wear to church."

Guinevere says "I will organize the church ladies to clean Walter's home and distribute his meager belongings to the needy.

Merlin and I will feed the animals at Walter's shack until they are picked up by their new owners. Petunia is coming back to stay with us for the time being.

Sunday morning is here and I am anxious to see Walter one last time. He is lying in the beautiful coffin with half the lid opened. The bottom of the coffin is covered with a new flag. Two soldiers in full dress uniform stand at attention on each end of the casket with rifles on their shoulders. There are so many bouquets of flowers in front of the platform that the honey bees will probably starve this fall. Walter is wearing King Arthur's Sunday suit. His hair is combed and his whiskers shaved making him look like a prosperous banker.

I wish they had left his whiskers on because I hardly recognize him. The entire congregation files by the casket and says goodbye. The soldiers close the lid on the coffin. They fold the flag into a small triangle and hand it to Merlin. They march side by side out the door of the church. They turn and fire their guns in the air a bunch of times causing the neighbor dogs to start howling.

When the soldiers leave, Merlin stands in front of Walter's casket and tells of his heroism in WWI. He holds up an old army shirt to show two rows of ribbons and medals. He speaks of Walter's loss of fiancée and father and mother and his leg.

He says "Walter was my best friend and I will miss Walter greatly.

He says "Walter was a recluse because he didn't want to burden others with his pain."

He says "Walter's soul is now and forever at rest."

Everyone present is weeping. One by one each member of the congregation tells of Walter's virtues. This outpouring of love amazes me because I thought everyone disapproved of the alcoholic recluse. I stand to remind everyone that Walter got saved and baptized last summer and we will all see him again in heaven but I'm not sure we will recognize him in his white robe and halo

244

singing with the saints. I realize that I never have heard Walter sing and wonder what he will sound like.

We all file out of the church lead by the pastor and six men carrying Walter in his casket. A hole was prepared in the churchyard cemetery and the casket is lowered to the bottom. The preacher preaches a wonderful sermon mainly reminding us that we too shall join Walter in death and must always be prepared. Every member of the congregation throws a chunk of dirt on the coffin and then the pall bearers grasp shovels to fill the grave with the dirt they removed while digging it. There is a lot more dirt that came out of that hole than can fit back in, so a large mound is built on top of the grave.

One by one, the congregation leaves the cemetery and gets into a car to drive home.

We are the last to leave.

LEGACY

Walter Noland died a month ago. I think of him often. Merlin and I laugh about leaving the car after I accidentally drove it away. We are careful not to talk about the exciting baptismal service around other church members as they might think we are making light of a Holy Sacrament. I told Merlin that Walter would have really enjoyed Communion if we did it right with real wine. We actually use Welch's grape juice at our church for communion. Today is the auction.

When the church ladies went to Walter's shack to put everything in order and clean the shack, they found a note on the table. The note in Walter's handwriting states that all of his worldly goods are to be given to Merlin except that his car is to be given to Sir Lancelot. It went on to apologize for drinking so much and dunking the preacher during his baptism. Merlin has already distributed the livestock to those who might appreciate each animal. Many pieces of old equipment are also distributed to surrounding neighbors. Now the remaining land and home are to be auctioned off. Merlin is donating the proceeds to the Salvation Army in superior.

Walter's Model T is sitting behind our tool shed. The armor bearers and I have been washing and sanding the rust off the old car until shiny metal can be seen here and there. King Arthur and Merlin cut some boards and fitted them in where the old floor boards had rotted through. We are going to the general store in Superior next Wednesday to buy paint. We will paint the Model T.

We discuss various paint schemes. The car will have at least two colors and we will paint a stripe around the doors. The doors don't open and the door handles are missing. Guinevere replaced the driver's box with a bench that stretches from one door to the other. She made a pad for the bench from colorful flour sacks and stuffed the pad with straw so it is as comfortable as the seat in the Buick and a whole lot prettier.

I stand on the bench seat at the steering wheel and tell of my first driving experience while the armor bearers stand in the back and sit on the bench seat beside me. We pretend we are driving a race car at Indianapolis. We pretend we are driving a fire truck. We pretend we are driving a police car. We twirl our arms in the air imitating a flashing red light and make siren sounds. I am an expert on siren sounds after the policeman demonstrated them to me in Superior when I was lost. We pretend we are driving an army tank. We make lots of gunfire sounds. This car is the best toy anyone has ever had.

Merlin has warned me that I cannot jack the rear tire off the ground and start the car as that could cause an accident. I'm not sure I could pull the crank hard enough to start the car anyway.

I know how to open the hood exposing the motor. I know how to check the oil and gas level and where to pour them in if needed. I wash the engine off with soap and water until it is sparkling clean. I will paint the motor as well as the outside of the car. I plan to drive this car for the rest of my life so I must take very good care of it.

Merlin says "The most important thing to do to keep a car in good shape is to change the oil often."

I have a wrench that I keep under the seat to loosen the oil plug on the bottom of the engine. Guinevere gave me an old porcelain wash basin to catch the oil in. I drain the oil into the wash basin and then replace the plug. I then pour the oil back into the engine from a Campbell's soup can with one side pinched together for a pouring spout. I sometimes change the oil in my car three times a week. I had to add an extra quart at the last oil change although the car can't be burning oil as we have only started it twice since bringing it home from the Noland place.

Merlin says we can drive my car to church next Sunday if it isn't raining. The Buick gets a bit crowded with three adults and seven kids even though it is a ginormous automobile. I think King Arthur and Guinevere will be riding in the Buick alone as all of the armor bearers want to ride in my car with Merlin Sunday.

I am the only first grader in our entire school with his own car. I remind classmates of my driving skill often. Some think I am making this stuff up, but we all know the truth. I really did take my car for a drive last summer. The car was given to me because I am a good driver. I am currently restoring the car and plan to drive it to school when I am done.

We head for Superior to get fencing materials and nails and paint for my car. I want to have Merlin drive my car, but he says it is better to keep the Model T on side roads close to home. We discuss paint colors and quantity and uses with the store keeper. He offers to give me several cans of paint that are half full. Guinevere said

248

we can only spend one dollar on paint for the car so we would be limited to one can of black paint. The free paint is an answer to psychedelic dreams. There are nine cans of various colored paint, some nearly half full. We carefully pack the paint into a box so it will not spill in the trunk of the Buick. Twenty cents buys two paint brushes and a can of turpentine with which to wash them out.

The car is beautiful. I painted the engine bright red with a yellow fan blade. Merlin said we shouldn't paint the radiator core as we might plug up the air flow and cause the engine to overheat, so that is still rusty brown. The hood is green as is the back bumper. The doors are blue and the wheel jack with its trip rope is yellow. The running boards are a very dark blue. The inside of the car is mostly brown, but we ran out of brown paint and part of the left side is maroon. A white pinstripe runs around the whole outside of the car. It is real hard to get the line exactly the same width everywhere and it is a bit wavy which only adds to its beauty. The crowning touch is the wheels. The wooden spokes of the wheels are each painted a different color. The spare tire attached to the back of the car is painted in the same manner. At first we tried to plan what color each part of the car would be, but we ran out of some colors and had extra of others so the paint job sort of just happened. Merlin said we should paint the tractor after he saw the nice job we did on Walter's Model T. King Arthur squelched that idea in a hurry. He said Farmall would reposses the tractor if we painted it like that, and it would scare the chickens.

Merlin starts my car and drives up to the door. It is Indian summer and the sun is shining. He is going to drive my older brother and I to school in my car. I washed the new paint job carefully last week so it is ready to go. I sit next to Merlin with my brother riding shotgun. I have my great notched sword in my hand and stand with my sword raised high as we tool on down the road. We don't have to take all the side roads to pick up other kids so the trip is a lot shorter than riding the bus. A crowd of excited classmates surrounds my car when we arrive. Merlin agrees to give everyone a ride in groups of eight. I stand in the back with my sword in the air and bring it down to signal time to start out with each load. I tell every group that I have driven my car all by myself, but Merlin is along today so he can bring the car back home when we are in school.

I tell everyone that a war hero, Walter Noland, drove this car for many years. When he died he gave the car to me and I intend to drive it for the rest of my life. Walter Noland's memory will not disappear as long as Sir Lancelot lives.

INTERIOR DECORATOR

It's raining cats and dogs this morning. King Arthur and Merlin put on their rain gear and head out to milk the cows and get the chores done before breakfast. I volunteer to lead the troops into the rain for egg collecting. We don't have rain coats, but we all put on two shirts and a jacket so we will be warm even if we do get wet. I and the two oldest armor bearers are finally outfitted for rain and start for the kitchen door with three egg baskets. Guinevere heads for the door ahead of us and reaches for the family umbrella stored behind the door.

I quickly point out that we will split up to gather the eggs to minimize our exposure to the weather. There is only one umbrella. Too late!

Guinevere says "At least one of you can stay dry."

She picks up the umbrella and attempts to open it. The jig is up! The last time that umbrella was opened was during our flying experiments where it was employed as a parachute. We straightened the ribs so good and wrapped it in its closed form so neatly that it looks undamaged. It has been standing behind the door ready to be discovered ever since. The day of reckoning is here!

Guinevere pushes the button on the handle of the umbrella. It should spring open actuated by a complicated spring mechanism. Nothing happens. The armor bearers and I move back for safety. We know exactly what is wrong with the umbrella. We hold our breath trying to gauge Guinevere's emotions as she struggles in an attempt to open the broken umbrella. She pushes the slide up the handle, but the umbrella doesn't open. Two or three bent and broken ribs fall out and the cloth canopy sags open revealing torn spots. Guinevere isn't angry as we suspect she might be. She is really puzzled. She finally gets the umbrella sort of opened and examines the torn cloth and bent and broken ribs.

We could pretend to be as surprised as she is and get away with our secret. Instead, I start to cry and confess "I accidently broke the umbrella a long time ago and meant to tell you about it but I was afraid you would be angry with me."

Guinevere hugs me and says "It's no big deal since we never use the umbrella anyway. You will just have to get wet while you collect the eggs."

I can't believe my good fortune. I have been worried about the secret of the damaged umbrella far a long time and felt twinges of guilt every time I noticed it standing behind the kitchen door. Confession is good for the soul! Be sure your sins will find you out! These words spoken over the dinner table now take on new meaning. I have carried the burden of intentional deception needlessly! I worried about the possible punishment that might accompany confession. Now it appears that I was just punishing myself with the load of guilt. I feel ten pounds lighter as I head out into the rain to collect eggs.

Merlin and King Arthur are standing next to the wood box taking off their wet slickers and overshoes when we arrive with the eggs. We spent some time in the chicken coop waiting for the rain to let up, but it never did. We hand the egg baskets to Guinevere and strip to our underwear which is still pretty dry. The kitchen is warm and the stove is hot, ready for preparation of eggs and ham and pancakes. All is well in the Kingdom of Johnson. Dry clothes and a hot breakfast can bring the sunshine indoors even when it is raining outside.

Merlin is half through his stack of pancakes with butter and syrup and strawberry jam when he notices the tattered umbrella lying in the corner of the kitchen. He looks hard at the umbrella and then toward the kitchen door where it is always kept.

He asks "Is that our umbrella?"

Guinevere nods assent. He studies it from across the room in puzzlement.

"What happened to the umbrella?" he asks. "I saw it yesterday and it looked fine. The wind isn't that strong this morning."

My sunshine is slipping behind a cloud. Our secret is about to be discovered all over again with all the uncertainty that brings. Mom can be stern but her discipline is never severe. Merlin has never uttered a harsh word to me or any of the armor bearers. I fear his displeasure more than any punishment and start to cry again. Merlin is really puzzled now. Even as he asks what is causing a fearless knight to cry, the armor bearers are all talking at once in an unintelligible cacophony of explanations involving flying experiments and intrigue.

Merlin raises his hands, palms down to slow everything down. He looks at me and asks "Were you trying to fly in the rain this morning?"

I confess "The flying experiments occurred a long time ago."

Merlin asks why the umbrella is just damaged this morning if the flying which caused it is in the distant past. Now the real problem is uncovered. The accidental damage could be excused as ignorance, though sneaking the umbrella out of the house has no reasonable defense. The subsequent cover-up is without excuse. King Arthur says Politicians get into more trouble with their cover-ups than they do with their stupid mistakes. Merlin says we should have a meeting of the round table tonight where the tales of attempted flight can be told and Sir Lancelot will be chastised by the King for dishonesty.

Did I mention that it is raining outside? The umbrella is discarded and forgotten. King Arthur is going over plans for next year's crop rotations and budgets for equipment and other farm related business with Merlin. Guinevere is reading a book next to the fireplace. Seven other inhabitants of the kingdom tire of playing "Thimble-Thimble, Who's got the Thimble". We request permission to play upstairs and receive it.

The possible hiding places for "Hide and Seek" are quickly exhausted and the space is too small for a game of "Tag". I know that idleness is the Devil's workshop, so I try to think of a project to keep everyone occupied. We decide to redecorate the boy's bedroom.

The planning alone requires a lot of discussion. The final plan involves moving the bed to a new position. It takes a lot of effort by all to move the heavy bed. The move creates a bit of noise and Guinevere comes up to investigate. She agrees that the change will be interesting and goes back to her book. We continue with

254

repositioning of the dresser and toy box. The ball is rediscovered and several new ball games are invented. This rainy day is turning out to be more fun than a day in the sun. We head right back upstairs after lunch before someone thinks of naps as a way to spend time.

The two smallest armor bearers have been coloring pictures. We decide that pictures on the wall will add to the décor. The ceiling is white and the walls are pale yellow. A few bright colors will pick the place up a lot. It is really hard to get the pictures to stay on the walls. I have a stroke of genius. There are six paint cans each with a little bit of bright colored paint in the basement left over from painting my car. We can paint bright designs on the wall for decoration. This will be a big surprise to be announced at the meeting of the Round Table tonight after supper.

Guinevere and King Arthur and Merlin are all sitting in the living room near the fireplace. They don't even notice us getting the paint and brushes from the basement. Guinevere asks if we would like a snack, but no one is hungry. They have prepared a pot of tea and are sipping the tea by the fireplace, completely unaware that we are about to redecorate the boy's room far beyond moving a bit of furniture.

The job is done exquisitely. We are able not only to make interesting designs on the walls with the original six colors, but we mix colors to create entirely new colors as well. My older brother is in second grade and prints very well. He prints each of the boy's names on the inside of the door and "Boy's Room" on the outside. It looks so nice that we move to the girl's room and decorate their door in a similar manner. We are on a roll. We paint Mom and Dad on their door. We are all out of paint so Merlin will have to identify his room some other way. We are unsure of how to spell "Merlin" anyway. We spend the rest of the afternoon trying to wipe up the paint that got spilled on the dresser and bed and floor. All in all, this is a job to be proud of. We can't wait until the announcement tonight at the Round Table.

Guinevere calls us down for supper. She is in the kitchen placing the macaroni and cheese on the table with a loaf of hot bread fresh from the oven. We will have Kool-Aid as a special treat tonight. We usually drink milk and water with supper. Guinevere places her hands on the sides of her head in surprise as we march into the kitchen. I am holding the great notched sword in the air leading the procession. The armor bearers follow in single file, arms swinging in unison. I bet the new bright yellow paint on my sword has caught her by surprise.

She calls Merlin and King Arthur to come quickly. We are lined up next to the kitchen table. My sword is at my side, but I raise it in salute as the King and Magician enter the room. They begin to laugh.

This is puzzling to the whole band of warriors. We look at each other and realize that we have a lot of paint on our faces and hands and clothes. I bet our redecoration announcement isn't going to wait until the meeting of the Round table.

WHAT'S WRONG WITH MERLIN?

Merlin is my uncle and father of four armor bearers. Two boys and two girls. The oldest of the girls is six like my older brother. They stair step down to three years old like my younger brother. Our families would be a matched pair for age if I had another sibling four years old like my youngest female cousin. It may seem strange to have these families living and working together on the Johnson farm, but the melding of our families into one large extended family came out of tragedy.

Merlin (Uncle Ralph) was employed by the Union Pacific Railroad as an engineer operating trains in Northern Wisconsin and Minnesota after returning from military service in Germany. He occasionally talks about life riding the rails, but never discusses his military experience. He was operating a train in North Dakota when my youngest cousin was born a month prematurely. My aunt died a few hours after the baby was born.

Uncle Ralph quit his job on the railroad that day and hitchhiked back to his home\in Superior to take care of his four children. Kenny was tough and clung to life tenaciously surviving six weeks of intensive care in the hospital. The hospital bills and other expenses rapidly consumed Uncle Ralph's savings and the bank foreclosed on his house. Unable to work and care for his family, he offered to work on the Johnson farm with his brother (King Arthur, my dad) until he could find other means to care for his family. It has been nearly three years that our families have enjoyed life together.

I sort of remember Uncle Ralph coming to live with us, but it seems like that is the way it has always been. Now things are getting a little weird. Uncle Ralph bought his own car even though the Buick sits in the driveway without being started for days at a time. Merlin can drive it anytime he wants. Besides, I have my own car and Merlin can drive it any time he likes as well. My car has some drawbacks since there is only the one bench seat with no back to sit on and the doors are welded shut and it has no top and it won't go more than thirty five without the front end shimmying a lot. I still change the oil at least every other week. My car is the prettiest car in the area sporting six or seven colors in all, with each spoke on the wooden wheels painted a different bright color. It runs like a new car but it is a little noisy since the muffler fell off. Merlin and I are the only ones that ever drive my car.

Merlin bought a Ford sedan with a flathead V-8 motor and lots of power. It isn't as big as the Buick, but it's close. Merlin opened the hood on his car and pointed at the air cleaner. He said" That's a four barrel carb under there and it puts real power in this machine. I can pass a truck easily. It has a trailer hitch and can pull the two wheeled trailer loaded to the hilt!"

I asked "Why do you need a car?"

He said "I will be able to drive to church without making everyone late if it takes too long to clean the milking equipment. I can take a friend to dinner in Spooner when your dad is getting supplies in Superior. Your mom and dad can take a trip to Minneapolis for the weekend and the rest of us will still have a car if we need it."

I said "I really like your car. The maroon paint is really shiny. I guess it is only fair that you have your own car just like I do. I have no real reason to own a car other than the fact that I like to have it. The kids at school are really envious of my car. Now we have three cars and a truck and two tractors on our farm. That is really something when you realize that only one other farm in the whole community has more than one car and a truck. The Swenson's second car doesn't even run.

Merlin grins and says "Trudy Erickson asked me to take her for a ride in my new car. What do you think about that?"

I answer "I think that is a great idea. Can I go along?"

Merlin says "I already told her I would pick her up after milking tonight. You would miss supper. It might be late by the time I get home and you need to get your sleep for school tomorrow."

I didn't hear him say NO, did you? I decided to talk about something else so he wouldn't scotch the plan beginning to hatch in my mind. I will go along for the ride, but I won't let them know so they can make me stay home. I'm not sure why, but it seems that Merlin is acting a bit strange. He may need my help. I bet I've heard Trudy Erikson's name on Merlin's lips twenty times in the last week.

Its: "Trudy graduated from the University of Wisconsin with honors." Trudy is the only lady I know who looks nice with short hair." "Trudy has read the entire Harvard Classics Series of more than thirty volumes." "Trudy speaks French." "Trudy this." "Trudy that." I know more about Trudy Erikson than I do about half of my relatives. I'm afraid Merlin is being smitten by the same spell I fell under when Violet entered my life. I was careful not to talk about Violet all the time to make it obvious like Merlin is doing now, making himself a fool over Trudy. He may need my help as I am the only one I know of who has experience in these matters.

I'm not good at lying, but I don't know how to execute my plan to save Merlin without a bit of subterfuge. Milking is done and King Arthur and Merlin come into the kitchen in a talkative mood. They are laughing on the way in from the barn. They might be going crazy. I've heard that craziness runs in families and I suppose that I might be crazy since I talked to a psychiatrist. Maybe I infected Merlin and King Arthur.

King Arthur goes into the bathroom to wash his hands for supper. He is in his stocking feet since he took off his barn clothes and is now wearing his house jeans and T shirt. Merlin leans over and kisses Guinevere on the cheek and says, "You have a delicious supper prepared but I will get something to eat with Trudy." He then steps into the bathroom and starts the bath water running as King Arthur emerges.

He says, "I think I'll take a bath before I go out tonight." Merlin then heads to his room taking the steps upstairs two at a time like he is in a hurry.

I say to no one in particular, "I'm not hungry! I think I'll go to bed early." I'm nearly knocked down the stairs by Merlin carrying his church clothes to the

260

bathroom where he will take a bath. I have plans of my own for this evening.

I get a blanket out of the closet and lift the bedroom window. I look around the room and realize that my absence will be obvious, so I quickly roll up another blanket and stuff it in bed and mess up the covers a little. Two pillows on top of each other make it look a little bit like someone is asleep in the bed. I put a note just under the covers where my brother will find it. It reads, "DON"T TELL." I lay my sword on the note next to the rolled up blanket.

This is a real loyalty test. I trust my brother not to tell on me, but if he does, the note will convince everyone that I was not kidnapped. Now, for the dangerous part of the plan. I broke the downspout last summer and it was never replaced. I have to escape out the window onto the porch roof and get to the ground. I'm not sure if Merlin's magic will protect me this time. I throw the blanket onto the lilac bush at the edge of the porch and leap into space. The lilac bush takes a beating as I land on the blanket and tumble to the ground unhurt. I hope no one notices the broken branches on the lilac bush.

I furtively climb into the back seat of Merlin's car and cover myself with the blanket on the floor behind the front seat. My heart is thumping so hard that I'm afraid Merlin will hear it when he gets in the car. I'm breathing hard as well because I hurried to get everything done while Merlin is taking his bath. If he moves as fast with that as he did getting his clothes running up and down the stairs, I know I don't have any time to spare. I am just able to get my breathing under control when the front door of the car opens.

Oh! No! I'm discovered. I feel Merlin's hand on the blanket over my head! The car engine roars to life. The radio begins to blare out a song by Hank Williams. "Your Cheating Heart Will Tell On You!" How does the guy on the radio know what I'm doing? The car lurches backward, stops and accelerates forward. I pull the cover off my head to see what is happening.

I'm safe! Merlin just threw his coat in the back seat and I thought it was his hand on my head. I cover back up and sense the car stopping at the bottom of the driveway. It then turns onto county B and accelerates a lot faster than I remember Merlin driving in the past. We stop and start and turn. I have no idea where we might be since I am on the floor under a blanket and coat. The car slows and turns onto gravel which crunches under the tires. The car stops and Merlin gets out, slamming the door behind him.

I cautiously rise up to look out the side window. I watch Merlin climb the porch steps on a strange house and knock on the door. Trudy answers the door and Merlin disappears into the house. Has he changed his mind about taking her for a ride in his new car? Neither of them even glances toward the car where I'm hiding in case I'm needed in an emergency. How can I help Merlin if he is in the house and I don't even know if he's in trouble? I'm considering sneaking into the house to see if everything is all right when the door opens and I dive back under the blanket.

Merlin opens the passenger door and Trudy slides in. Something is up because she slides to the middle of

262

the seat. Is someone else coming along? Will there be so many that someone has to ride in the back seat? I am really in a pickle now!

The door shuts and no one else gets in. The driver's door then opens and Merlin slides into the car, slamming the door. He unlatches the seat and slides it back several inches, nearly squashing me. Trudy's perfume fills the car. She is giggling but no one is saying anything funny. The motor roars to life and the radio blares out a silly love song. Trudy turns the volume down a bit and begins to sing along. Merlin joins in. I've never heard Merlin sing like that before. At least not with this much enthusiasm! He does sing in church and when the preacher comes over to sing after supper, but it has always been more restrained. He is sitting in the front seat belting out a love song as he backs the car out of the driveway.

We are back on the road with a stop and turn now and then followed by a long stretch of steady driving. Trudy asks about each member of our family and Merlin tells her about us like we have no flaws. She laughs out loud when he tells her about the redecorated the bedrooms. She literally shrieks with laughter when he describes his reaction to our haircuts. My hair is a couple of inches long now and I think I will abandon the bald look.

Trudy gets real quiet when Merlin starts describing his wife's death and his baby's first precarious days. He says, "It took over a day to get home and I had no idea what was happening to my family. I found Eunice (my mom) taking care of the kids and Kenny just barely alive and Sally was gone. I tried to take care of everyone but nearly gave up when the bank served the foreclosure notice on me. My brother said he would like to make my house payments, but the farm provided just enough to stay solvent. One bad crop could result in the farm being foreclosed. I couldn't sleep and had nightmares about the Germans invading Superior. I started drinking a bit of whiskey just to sleep and found that even a lot of whiskey didn't help me get any rest or peace. Walter Noland came to visit and cursed me for trying to take the easy way out. He said he did the same as I was doing but he didn't have any family to take care of. Walter said he had hoped he would die from his drinking but it hadn't worked that way. He said that he would take an axe and chop one of my legs off if he ever caught me drunk again. Then I would at least have a lame excuse for my drinking. Walter was the only one that really understood my despair because he had been there himself."

I'm hungry. I wish I had at least gotten a bite of the supper I turned down. My stomach is growling. I will be discovered if the noise of the car stops. The car does finally stop and Merlin gets out of the car and opens Trudy's door to let her out. He then reaches into the back seat and grabs his coat. I can't believe he doesn't see the blanket on the floor but he must be distracted by that perfume.

I rise up to look out the window and see a store front with the letters "CAFE" in neon in the window. I can't see inside the building so I cover back up with my blanket to wait for Merlin and Trudy to return after they eat.

Suddenly, Merlin is shaking my shoulder. He says "Wake up! We're home!" It is pitch black outside. We are parked in the driveway of the Kingdom of Johnson. Trudy isn't in the car any more. Merlin reaches into the back seat of the car and picks me and the blanket up in a wad and carries me to the house. I am awake by the time we reach the porch and I walk into the house with him. We sit at the kitchen table. Merlin pours me a glass of milk and heats himself some cold coffee left over from supper.

He asks, "Are you hungry? Did you get any supper?"

I answer, "I'm starved!"

Merlin slices a thick piece of bread from the loaf and slathers butter, peanut butter and strawberry preserves on it. I have never tasted a better sandwich!

Merlin asks, "Why did you go to all that trouble just for a ride in my new car?"

I said, "I was worried that you weren't thinking clearly. I was afraid you would get into some kind of trouble with Trudy since it seems like she is all you have been thinking about lately. I know how girls can mess with your head since I have had that same problem myself."

Merlin laughs, "You are right! I asked Trudy to marry me tonight. If you had stayed awake you might have prevented that."

I said, "I'm not going to ask Violet to marry me, but I am willing to wear her scarf as I go on a dangerous mission. Did Trudy know I was in the car? Is she mad at me? Did she agree to marry you?"

Merlin put his hands out, palms down and moved them up and down. He said, "Slow down partner! One thing at a time! First, don't be so sure what you are going to do in the future. I agree with your decision to not marry Violet just now, but don't let that prevent a change of mind in the future. Trudy doesn't know you were riding along with us, nor did I until I decided to carry that blanket in from the floor of the car when we arrived home. You must have slept through most of our trip or you would know the answer about Trudy agreeing to marry me. I wouldn't even mention asking if she had turned me down."

I said, "Now I understand why you loved Walter Noland."

Merlin said, "Walter saved my life when I didn't think there was anything left to save. I wish I could have benefited Walter in the same way. You came closer to meeting Walter's need when you helped him accept his eminent death. Walter helped me regain my life and I gave him respect. None of us can make it without the rest of us. Always remember that when one hand washes the other, both are cleaner. Where's your sword? Did you leave it home when you were out on one of your most important missions?"

I said, "I left it in bed with a note for my brother so he wouldn't tell what I was up to."

Merlin said, "The sword is right where it needs to be. Use all of your tools wisely and the outcomes will be good. Let's keep it a secret that you came along for our ride tonight. Trudy and I talked about very personal

266

things for a long time and she might be embarrassed. She doesn't know how sound you sleep. What do you think of her?

I said, "I like her and she smells good. That doesn't really matter though. What do you think of her?"

Merlin answered, "I love her."

I replied, "I thought so from the way you sing together."

THE KINGDOM CRUMBLES

Merlin and King Arthur are on the way to the house after milking. They are laughing and punching each other on the shoulder and generally acting like kids that just won a baseball game. King Arthur takes off his barn coat and boots in the entry room and walks over to Guinevere before he even washes up for breakfast. He wraps his arms around her and bends her back for a big kiss. This is really weird since Guinevere is easily embarrassed and King Arthur is usually very reserved.

King Arthur laughs and announces "We will have to start looking for a hired hand. Ralph says he plans to quit farming and return to train driving." Guinevere is caught off guard. She puts her hands to her hair to fix where King Arthur messed it up. She asks, "When did this all come about? How come I didn't know anything about these plans? When will this all happen?"

Merlin chimes in, "John and I have been talking about the possibility for the past four months. Union Pacific offered my job back. I will be training new engineers as well as providing backup on runs where a senior engineer is needed to fill in temporarily. The job offers a substantial salary increase and I will be able to supplement the farm income if finances get tight here. I will start the first of the year. I didn't talk to anyone about it until now because I didn't know if I could accept the job and still care for the kids. Last night, Trudy agreed to marry me and take care of the kids. We will live in Superior where she will begin writing a book she has been working on. I won't miss cleaning the barn, but

I will sure miss your cooking. Lets sit down to breakfast and enjoy a bit if that right now."

Guinevere cuts thick slices of bread from the loaf while she asks "When do you plan to marry?"

Merlin laughs as he replies "Why are you asking me? Trudy told me to mind my own business when I asked the same question. She says the bride gets to plan the wedding but I had better have a place to stay by Christmas. I recommend that any questions about weddings be brought to Trudy. Last night I suggested that we take a trip to Judge Nelson's house as soon as she agreed to marry me. She said that wouldn't be a proper wedding and she plans to wear her mom's wedding dress because her mom has saved that dress for her for over twenty five years."

King Arthur sits down to breakfast and we all take our seats around the table and join hands. He usually thanks God for food and requests guidance for the day. Today he thanks God for so much stuff that the food is getting cold. I peek to see when he will be done and see him wiping a tear from his face. I shut my eyes again real quick so he won't know I saw the tear.

We eat a hearty breakfast with everyone talking at once. Marvin and I have to hurry, grabbing our lunch bags and heading for the bus. We sit together on the bus. We usually sit in different seats, me in the back telling tales of great adventure and him sitting with his friends talking about plans for recess and trading lunch items. Today we huddle together and discuss the implications of the wedding announcement. Marvin speculates that he will get his own room when our cousins move to

Superior. I suggest that he should get the girl's room. He asks "Who will get to keep our ball since we bought it together?" I suggest," We should give it to our cousins as a wedding gift." He agrees.

Merlin announces that he will be having supper with Trudy. He says, "Trudy asked me to bring Jane and Dennis and Amy and Kenny along. We will get back in time for bed."

Marvin and Lyle and I see an ominous sign. Our Families are dividing. I don't even ask if I can come. The changes on the horizon are going to turn the Kingdom of Johnson on its ear. Dennis begins to cry and says "I'm not going! I don't even like Trudy! Can we just tell her we changed our minds?"

Jane and Amy huddle together with their arms around each other. They excitedly discuss what they can bring to share with Trudy. Jane says "We have two jars of choke cherry jelly left. Can we take one for supper tonight?"

Guinevere says, "That is the best use I can think of for our prize jelly. We will save the other one for a wedding present." She tells Merlin, "I will be planning a wedding shower Tuesday next week. That will give us time to announce the engagement and invite people to the shower at church next Sunday."

We all go out to the porch and wave goodbye to Merlin and most of my armor bearers as they pile into the Ford. No one says a word. We stand quietly on the porch and watch the car move down the driveway and out onto County Road B. It finally disappears around the corner. I think Walter's funeral was a happier parting than watching Merlin and the armor bearers leave for dinner at Trudy's house.

The enormity of the change swirling about us settles in. We will be able to visit, but living together is a whole other thing. We turn and re-enter a house that suddenly seems empty. There is no chatter and pushing as we gather around the table for supper. Mom has gone to special effort preparing one of our favorite dishes. A loaf of fresh bread is cooling on the shelf next to the stove. A thick cheese sauce using lots of cream and butter and a bit of flour is poured over the kettle of boiled macaroni. A special touch is added tonight with finely diced onion and tiny cubes of ham stirred into the macaroni and cheese.

We sit quietly at the table and join hands like we did this morning. There are now five instead of ten participants. Dad bows his head and prays, "Dear Lord, be with Ralph and the children as they organize their new family. Help them to learn to love each other as much as we love them. Set their feet on solid ground and direct their paths. ...."

A long silence follows. I look up even though I don't hear an "Amen". Tears are flowing down dad's cheeks. Mom is dabbing at her eyes. My brothers are watching as well. We don't pretend not to notice the emotions flowing around the table. I ask, "Dad, are you crying because Uncle Ralph and His family plan to move to superior?"

Dad says, "I will miss my brother and his family, but these are tears of joy. When Ralph came to stay with us, he thought his life was over. Now he is leaving with hope in his heart. We healed his hurt by inviting him to Camelot where we all lived in royal splendor. I don't understand how Camelot came to exist here on the Johnson farm, but you all played a role in its creation.

Marvin asks," Can we eat now? I notice that you forgot to thank God for the food and this is pretty good stuff. I wonder if Trudy is a good cook. We will have to get a read on that when they get back tonight."

As we dig into the Macaroni and cheese, the reflection on our loss is swallowed up in all kinds of silly talk. I suggest, "If Merlin retains his special magic, he can make a palace in Superior where we can visit." Marvin observes," We won't be able to hear the stories Uncle Ralph reads to us at night. I will read them if you will help me with the hard words." Lyle says," I think we need to start by reading 'Tom Sawyer' again and I will be Huck Finn. One of you can be Tom Sawyer and Violet can be Becky." I chime in," I guess that makes me Tom Sawyer because I have a special relationship with Violet." Marvin says," Let us make the woods into the wilderness and I can be Daniel Boone." Dad says, "Why not try being the Johnson family living on a farm in northern Wisconsin. That is a story that can be invented as we live it. It will match any of the stories you are talking about. The country Johnson family can visit the city Johnson family in Superior where we can swap stories and enjoy each other's company.

I hang the great notched sword on a nail over my bed to remind me of the days when I was Sir Lancelot. I feel good to be going into the future as one of the country Johnson kids. That is the title I will carry to my grave.

ABOUT THE AUTHOR

Arnold Orvin Hopland was born in Chicago, IL October 1, 1944 to a family struggling for economic survival. A move to Cass Lake, MN followed in a few months, where his father's family lived. His father, Orvin Arnold Hopland, obtained one short term job followed by another as the family moved to Fargo, ND, Bemedji, MN, Lacrosse, WI, Superior, WI, St Paul, MN, Lake Nebagamon, Wi, Wentworth, WI, Poplar, WI, Hawthorn, WI, Lima Center, WI, Old Johnstown, WI, Janesville, WI, Footville, WI, back to Old Johnstrown, and then Janesville, WI, where his father died from a surgical mishap during a back surgery. The Hopland family found inexpensive housing squatting in abandoned or low value houses where water was obtained by hand pump from a shallow well and outhouses were the height of sanitation facilities. When no work was available, a rent increase to $10 or $20 monthly from nothing or part time labor trade out might require relocation. Arnold attended 16 different grade schools with a brother, Marvin, one year older and another brother, Lyle, two years younger.

The effect of this nomadic existence resulted in exceptional adaptation skills. Arnold weighed less than 50 pounds at 8 years of age, but held his own in schoolyard scraps where a local bully attempted to teach him respect at each new location. Arnold never initiated confrontation, but made physical confrontations so painful to bullies that they didn't often attempt a second confrontation. Books substituted for friends. His mother, June Edna Liljegren, lost use of her right arm in a childhood accident and overcame that handicap without complaint, though she was limited in her ability to care for her struggling family. She married Joseph Roush 2 years after Orvin's death. He was a nearly destitute sharecropper who was required to declare bankruptcy and sell his obsolete farm equipment and small herd of cows within a year of the marriage.

The common stepfather/stepson conflicts resulted in Arnold leaving home for farmhand employment at 14 years of age. Arnold attended high school in Milton, WI and graduated from Janesville, WI High school in 1962. Arnold studied electrical engineering at General Motors Institute under a work/study program obtaining a baccalaureate degree in Electrical Engineering. Philosophical interest prompted study at Bethel Theological Seminary for a year while he was employed by Univac Federal Systems Division to work on the Sentinel Antiballistic Missile System. The program was mothballed due to the antiballistic missile treaty with the USSR. Arnold then took a position with Gillman Engineering, designing automation equipment and obtained a Professional Engineering license from the state of Wisconsin. He also obtained a Master's degree in Business Administration from the University of Wisconsin. After promotion to project engineer, Arnold left the company to provide engineering consulting services and teach management and data processing at the University of Wisconsin. Pressure to obtain a PhD from academic administration resulted in a decision to attend medical school. With three children and a wife of ten years (high school sweetheart; the former Regina B. Davis), the family moved into cramped student housing facilities At the University of Wisconsin, where teaching business full time and medical school studies were combined. When a medical school professor discovered that Arnold was teaching as well as studying, he forced resignation from teaching duties. A fourth child was born to the Hopland family during the first year of medical school completing the nuclear family with Steven first, Jeffrey, second, Jennifer, third and finally, Kenneth completing the family. Aggressive investing, frugal lifestyle, and home renovations provided income during those lean years.

A year in Ancon, Panama as a medical intern at the Gorgas US Army Hospital provided exciting new cultural experiences and sailing adventure. This is the first time since teen years that Arnold held only one job with no school attached. An Intern's 60-70 hour work schedule seemed like part time employment to one whose life consisted of full time studies and full time work simultaneously. The next thirty five years are spent practicing medicine in Tennessee and Virginia, first in Emergency Medicine and then in Family Practice. Arnold immediately obtained a pilot's license advancing to instrument multiengine ratings with thousands of hours of flight time. Dr Hopland and his four children as partners have built a large medical practice with three clinic locations and over thirty employed providers. His oldest son, Steve, is CEO, Jeff (MD) is Medical Director, Jenny is board member, Kenny (MD) schedules providers and Arnold continues to see patients on a reduced schedule, serve on the board, and enjoy his wife of 50 years and fifteen grandchildren ranging from toddlers to college graduates.

Arnold's book "Sir Lancelot Tales" is his first work to be prepared for publishing. Now that the painful editing and re writing process has been completed for this material, more material now existing in rough draft form may get forced through that sausage grinder. You will greatly influence that decision through your feedback on this first attempt.